The **FATHERLESS** Journey for Guys

A 30 Day Devotional over the Fatherless Mountain

Sean P. Teis

Life Factors Ministries
spreading hope for life

The Fatherless Journey For Guys
A Devotional Journey Over the Fatherless Mountain

© 2011 Life Factors Ministries
Sean P. Teis

ISBN: 978-0-9832039-5-7

Photography by Valerie Sanders

The quoted ideas expressed in this book (but not Scripture verses) are not, in all cases, exact quotations, as some have been edited for clarity and brevity. In all cases, the author has attempted to maintain the speaker's original intent. In some cases, quoted material for this book was obtained from secondary sources, primarily print media. While every effort was made to ensure the accuracy of these sources, the accuracy cannot be guaranteed. For additions, deletions, corrections, or clarifications in the future editions of this text, please write:

Life Factors Ministries
P.O. Box 213, Duncansville, PA 16635

info@lifefactors.org
www.lifefactors.org

Scripture quotations are taken from: The King James Version

Printed in the United States of America

Faithful Life Publishers and Printers
North Fort Myers, FL 33903

www.FaithfulLifePublishers.com
info@FLPublishers.com

18 17 16 15 14 13 12 11   1 2 3 4 5

THE FATHERLESS JOURNEY

TO

_____

FROM

_____

DATE

_____

The Fatherless Journey

DEDICATION

This book is dedicated to a few deserving individuals, that without them I would not be here today. First, I dedicate this book to my wife and children, who have been extremely gracious in patience and support throughout all of my endeavors; their love, help, and encouragement have been the sustenance throughout this journey! Secondly, I dedicate this book to my mother, who was persistent in love throughout all of the hardships on my fatherless journey! Thirdly, I dedicate this book to my maternal grandparents, whose impact on my life through love and encouragement helped me begin my fatherless journey on a successful path! Fourthly, I dedicate this book to my mentor Jim and his family, who gave me much of the guidance and strength that I needed throughout my fatherless journey! I love you all and am extremely grateful! Lastly, but most importantly, I want to thank my Lord and Saviour, Jesus Christ for being my strength and guidance yesterday, today, and forever.

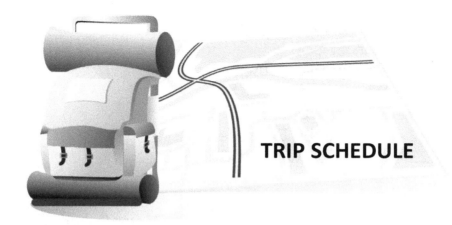

TRIP SCHEDULE

Preparation

Day 1 – Your Heavenly Father
Day 2 – So, You Are Fatherless
Day 3 – Facing the Facts
Day 4 – Talking to God
Day 5 – You Are Not Alone
Day 6 – You Are Loved
Day 7 – Consequences for Not Climbing
Day 8 – Overcoming Fear
Day 9 – Dealing with Discouragement

The Trip – Week 1 – The Incline (Internal Change)

Day 10 – Forgiveness
Day 11 – Inferiority
Day 12 – Trusting God
Day 13 – Uncontrolled Anger
Day 14 – Fearfully & Wonderfully Made
Day 15 – Self Esteem
Day 16 – Giving It All to God

The Trip – Week 2 – The Peak (External Change)

Day 17 – Submission to Authority
Day 18 – Man of God
Day 19 – Man of the House
Day 20 – Women
Day 21 – Being the Leader
Day 22 – Learning by Example
Day 23 – Manhood without Guidance

The Trip – Week 3 – The Summit (Your Future)

Day 24 – Be Confident
Day 25 – Mentors Part 1
Day 26 – Mentors Part 2
Day 27 – Father's Day
Day 28 – Character
Day 29 – Work Ethic
Day 30 – Success

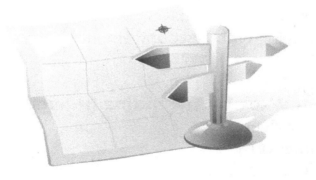

WELCOME

Dear Friend,

Welcome to the Fatherless Mountain! Most likely you did not decide to come to this mountain or volunteer to go on this journey, but for some reason out of your control, some circumstance brought you to this position in your life. When you became fatherless, regardless of how young you were, the feelings you had were probably equal to someone placing a backpack on your back with a ton of bricks in it and making you begin to climb. Included in this journey there were no instructions, no time estimation, and really not much help at all. So, now you are here, at the bottom of the mountain, you may feel all alone, looking at this mountain and thinking to yourself, how will I climb this thing?

Well there is good news; this devotional is designed to help you along your individual journey. There are certain issues you are facing or will come to face being fatherless and they need to be addressed. You need preparation, because the trip is not going to be easy, and it is not always fun, but with a little help and guidance you can make it through. I did it, and I have several friends that have as well. I have taken the knowledge of my personal experience and have polled others and in the next 30 days we will focus on working through the key elements that will most likely bog you down on your journey.

CHOICES – CHOICES – CHOICES!

So, now you are at your individual fatherless mountain looking up and staring at this monumental task and instantly the following two choices are made available to you:

> 1. You can lie down and be defeated and never climb over this mountain, dealing with the consequences for the rest of your life.
> **-OR-**
> 2. You can start climbing, conquer this life circumstance, and put this mountain behind you!

That is right; it is your decision. You as an individual decide what path you will take for the rest of your life, and you must get through this journey in order to move on.

You cannot ignore it, because it is staring you right in the face. To live a successful life you must confront this situation and begin dealing with it, and I hope that you will. I am positive you will make the right decision, and I cannot wait until I see you on the other side of this mountain. Have a great trip!

Oh, I almost forgot to mention, you will not be going on this trip alone. Paul will be your guide. He has experience with this mountain and even personally had to climb over it at the same age that you are right now. Each day Paul will share some insight on that day's specific topic. He will show you that since he got through it, you can too. He is ready, excited, and waiting to go on this trip with you!

You too have the ability to conquer this mountain and continue on successfully with the rest of your life. What are you waiting for? Go ahead and begin with day 1. I will be praying for you!

Your Friend,

Sean Teis
President
Life Factors Ministries

P.S. If you have any questions or need help along your journey please contact me through email at seanteis@lifefactors.org or on Facebook at http://www.facebook.com/SeanTeis, and I will try my best to help.

The Fatherless Journey

MYFATHERLESSJOURNEY.ORG

Life Factors Ministries created myfatherlessjourney.org as a website specifically designed to meet the needs of all fatherless girls/guys, single moms/guardians, and mentors. We are here for you and want to help you along your fatherless journey! Check the site out today!

MEET PAUL

Dear Friend,

I am so excited to finally meet you. I know that Sean had mentioned me to you, but I wanted to speak with you myself before Day 1. The trip that you are about to venture on will be exciting, but it will not be easy. I am confident that you will be able to conquer the certain areas in your life that will need improvement, and I want you to know that I will be with you throughout the entire trip. I will share with you some insight into my personal fatherless journey with hope that it will help and encourage you. I look forward to talking to you on Day 1.

-Paul

PREPARATION

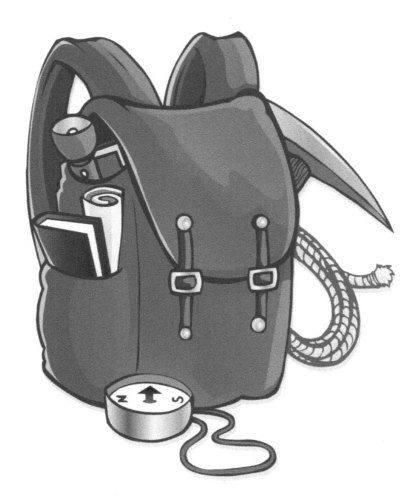

Days 1-9

The Fatherless Journey

Day 1

<u>Your Heavenly Father</u>

"For God so loved the world, that He gave His only begotten Son, that whosoever believeth in Him should not perish, but have everlasting life." John 3:16

The most amazing information that anyone has ever shared with me was the fact that God sent His only Son to this world to save me from my sins. The most important decision that I ever made was asking Jesus Christ into my heart as my personal Savior. How wonderful it is to know for sure that I will go to Heaven when I die. You too have the ability to decide where you will go when you die. If you have never accepted Christ as your personal Savior, follow the steps on the next page in the challenge section. Your decision of where you will spend eternity is the most important decision that you will ever make.

-Paul

CHALLENGE – DAY 1

Where you will go when you die is the most important decision you will ever make. That is right; it is your decision. You also get to decide whether or not you want a relationship with your Heavenly Father. You most likely did not decide to be fatherless, but now you have a chance to reconcile that event by seeking your Heavenly Father. The first step on the Fatherless Journey is confirming that you have a relationship with the Lord Jesus Christ. God wants you to rest in Him as your Heavenly Father. He will never leave, and He will never forsake you (Hebrews 13:5). All you must do is accept His Son, the Lord Jesus Christ as your personal Saviour. John 3:16 above shows that God loved us so much that He made a way for us to go to Heaven by sending His only begotten Son. The following verses will show you how to accept this free gift that He is offering to you:

> 1. Romans 3:23 – You must realize that you are a sinner. Have you ever lied, cheated, used a curse word, or disrespected your elder? If so, then you have sinned before, and admitting you are a sinner is the first step. Every person has sinned.
> 2. Romans 6:23a – The punishment for your sin is eternal death in Hell.
> 3. Romans 5:8 – Out of God's love for us, He sent His Son to die for our sins. This is our hope, through Christ we can be saved from an eternal death.
> 4. Romans 6:23b - God's gift is eternal life in Heaven through Jesus Christ.
> 5. Romans 10:13 – You must accept the gift by faith believing in Jesus and asking Him to come into your heart. If you understand this information and would like to ask Jesus into your heart, please pray the suggested prayer below.

 ## ACTION - In My Prayer Journal

In your first prayer journal entry write out a thank you letter to God for sending His Son to die for your sins.

Suggested Prayer: Dear Lord Jesus I know that I am a sinner. I know that You are God, and I know that You died in my place to pay for my sin. I believe that You rose from the dead, proving that You are God. Right now, in the best way that I know how, I call upon You and ask You to be my Lord and my Savior and my God. Thank You Jesus for dying for me. Help me now to live for You. Amen.

The Fatherless Journey

The Fatherless Journey

Day 2

So, You Are Fatherless

"Not that I speak in respect of want: for I have learned, in whatsoever state I am, therewith to be content." Philippians 4:11

Being fatherless and realizing that you are fatherless are two completely different factors. I was fatherless for quite some time before I finally realized that I needed to do something about being fatherless. I could not just relax with my life and become one of the failing statistics. I was strolling along in my life after realizing I was fatherless and I came across an interesting book called Fathers of Influence. This book was very intriguing to me as a fatherless individual, and in it I found the following quote to be very interesting:

> "Our fathers, while they can be as nurturing and gentle as our mothers, have been entrusted by God with a far different task. Theirs is the responsibility to help us make something of ourselves, to teach us by word and example how to be strong, hardworking, trustworthy, responsible men and women of character. Even for those who succeed only in part, the results can be astonishing, influencing generations."[1]

This quote was great for individuals blessed with fathers, but what about me, I asked to myself? I had to learn to find ways to be content with my situation. I had to accept the fact that I was indeed fatherless. This is an ongoing process that you too will need to continually work on. I challenge you today give this entire journey to the Lord.

-Paul

CHALLENGE – Day 2

The quote that Paul shared with you can be disheartening. You may be asking yourself several questions such as: Who will challenge you to be hardworking and trustworthy? Who will help you make something of yourself? Who will teach you to be a knowledgeable man with integrity? The reality is that you may not have someone to consistently teach you as this quote states, but you have been given a unique life path. You have been given the opportunity to learn from several men a wide variety of life lessons. You have been given independence and trust in many areas of your life and in the many decisions that you will face. Being fatherless is not a fun situation, and it definitely is hard to manage, but you can get through it. As you prepare for this journey, start thinking about satisfaction. What are the things in your life that you could be thankful for? What are things in your life that could be worse? You must accept the situation that you have been given and learn to be content. Follow what Paul shared in the following verse and begin to practice contentment in whatever life may bring: Philippians 4:11 "Not that I speak in respect of want: for I have learned, in whatsoever state I am, therewith to be content."

 ACTION - In My Prayer Journal

Write out the things that you have in your life to be thankful for. Remember that your life can always be in a worse state than it currently is.

Suggested Prayer: Dear God, I thank You today for the blessings that You have given to me. Help me to be content in this fatherless situation of my life. Help me to be thankful for the things that You have given to me and not to worry about the things I am missing. Amen.

The Fatherless Journey

The Fatherless Journey

Day 3

<u>Facing the Facts</u>

"And if children, then heirs; heirs of God, and joint-heirs with Christ; if so be that we suffer with Him, that we may be also glorified together. And we know that all things work together for good to them that love God, to them who are the called according to His purpose." Romans 8:17, 28

The facts of being fatherless are scary stuff! Check out some of the statistics that are being said about you and me:

> 1. 90% of homeless and runaway children are from fatherless homes.[2]
> 2. 63% of youth suicides are from fatherless homes.[3]
> 3. 71% of high school dropouts come from fatherless homes.[4]
> 4. 85% of youths in prisons grew up in a fatherless home.[5]
> 5. 80% of rapists motivated with displaced anger come from fatherless homes.[6]

After finding these statistics I am very thankful that I did not become one of them. It sure did get old being labeled with these facts when I was on my journey, and I am sure that you feel the same way. One of the most important aspects of this journey is realizing that you do not have to become a statistic, and actually, you have a chance to change the statistics. I overcame every statistic above and I challenge you to do the same.

-Paul

CHALLENGE – Day 3

These facts are very shocking and could be influential in your life. The true fact is that you have the opportunity to not become one of the statistics. The act of a father leaving is very detrimental to anyone's state of being. It has most likely affected your actions, attitude, thought process, and many other attributes of your life. After becoming fatherless, the most important necessity is to rely on God to get you through it. The wonderful thing about being a Christian is that you do not have to become a statistic. Romans 8:17 shows us that though we may suffer certain obstacles on this world, we have the hope of someday being "glorified together" in Heaven. Following this in verse 28 we are shown that "All things work together for good to them that love God." The individuals who compete in the Special Olympics are people of all ages who had the facts stacked against them. Many are labeled as disabled or handicapped, but this label does not stop them from pursuing their dreams of being an athlete. Some have an intellectual disability, others have a physical deformity, and the Special Olympics is a way for them to display their willingness to persevere despite their disabilities. You have not chosen to be a fatherless statistic, but you have the ability to be who God wants you to be on this earth regardless of the statistics that you may face. You may suffer in this world being fatherless, but if you live for the Lord despite your circumstances, glory will eventually come and all things will work together. Through your relationship with Jesus Christ you are able to conquer the biggest obstacles in the world.

 ## ACTION - In My Prayer Journal

Write out a challenge for yourself of how you will not become one of the statistics. Challenge yourself with goals that can be easily accomplished. Continuously look back at your goals and confirm that you are still achieving them.

Suggested Prayer: Dear Lord, thank You for giving me hope in You, and that despite the circumstances I may face on this earth I will be glorified together with You someday. I thank You for giving me the understanding that all things will work together through You. Please give me strength to face the facts of this trial in my life. Amen.

The Fatherless Journey

The Fatherless Journey

Day 4

Talking to God

"The effectual fervent prayer of a righteous man availeth much."
James 5:16b

My entire life I have gotten into trouble for talking. Not that I was saying anything inappropriate in my conversation, but because I was talking when I was not supposed to. In kindergarten, I got into trouble for talking during class. It did not stop there, from kindergarten up through my college days of school there were instances when I would get called out or held after class for talking. I guess I am what they call a "social bug." I love to talk. Even at work I was scolded on occasion for "socializing excessively". I am not at all proud of these scolding's at school or work, but they happened. To change, I had to go against my natural desire to be a "social bug" by striving to refrain from socializing at inappropriate times. I can honestly say that I have improved over the years, but it is still a constant struggle. All throughout my fatherless journey I am glad that I had God to talk to. No matter who was there or who was not there, He was always available to listen to me. At times the journey was lonely, but I could talk to Him, and I could hear Him talk to me through the reading of His Scriptures. I would not have made it through the journey without God's listening ear. I challenge you today to talk to God through your journey. I promise it will make the trip much easier!

-Paul

CHALLENGE – Day 4

Today there are multiple resources for communication. We can email, chat, text, talk on the phone, twitter, communicate on social sites such as Facebook and/or MySpace, and many other avenues. With all of these resources at our fingertips there are times when we still may feel like we have no one to talk to. Do you ever just want someone to talk to? Why not talk to God? Talking to God is simple. You don't have to log in, dial a number, or click send, but rather you just have to begin speaking to Him. He is always there, and He is always willing to listen to you. David is a great Biblical example of someone that continuously talked to God through the good and the bad times of life. The book of Psalms is filled with conversations that David had with God. These conversations reveal David's ups and downs in his life. Some Psalms are happy and some are sad. The Bible shows us in I Samuel 13:14 and Acts 13:22 that David was a man after God's own heart. David loved to talk to God. David was not perfect, but he laid his burdens down at God's feet. What about you? Who do you talk to in the good and bad times? Who will you talk to in the times to come? James 5:16b tells us that "The effectual fervent prayer of a righteous man availeth much." This means that talking to God will bring into your life great gain.

 ## ACTION - In My Prayer Journal

Write a note to God thanking Him for the things He has done and is doing in your life. Talk to Him about your burdens and problems. Look back at this note often and see what God has done in your life.

Suggested Prayer: Dear Lord, I thank You for loving me and giving me the ability to call upon You as often as I need. I ask that You would guide me as I begin to talk to You more. Please give me strength to get through my fatherless struggles, realizing that You are always there to listen to me. Amen.

The Fatherless Journey

The Fatherless Journey

Day 5

You Are Not Alone

"Let your conversation be without covetousness; and be content with such things as ye have: for He hath said, I will never leave thee, nor forsake thee."
Hebrews 13:5

When I was on my journey I did not have a guide to help me. That is why I have given my life to go on this journey with fellow fatherless friends. Have you thought about what will happen after you have finished this devotional book and I am not there to guide you anymore? One important item I want you to not forget is that you are not alone. Repeat after me, "I Am Not Alone." If you followed Day 1 or previously asked Jesus into your heart, you will never be alone. You and I have a friend in Jesus that is always there. No matter what time of the day we can talk to him, ask him for comfort, and seek advice from Him. Jesus loves you and wants you to succeed on this journey! When I was in high school attending youth group one night my youth pastor told us an interesting story. Here is a summary of that story:

His father was on a mission's trip in Haiti. They were driving through the jungle one night in a pickup truck. His father was in the back of the pickup truck. Suddenly several Haitian natives appeared from out of nowhere and began to surround their vehicle. These natives where chanting evil sayings. It was evident that these men were evil and were out to destroy these missionary workers. In fear and trembling the missionaries began singing "There Is Power in the Blood." These evil natives, now pressed up against the vehicle, began to back away and in an instance they disappeared.

Though I heard this story such a long time ago it still amazes me, because it shows that God is always with us. It proves that no matter how alone you or I may feel we are actually not alone at all. As Christians, God is always here. We have the Power of the Blood of Jesus Christ to get us through anything. I challenge you today to rest in the Power of the Blood.

–Paul

CHALLENGE – Day 5

Do you ever feel like you are all alone on your own personal island, as if no one understands you and your situation, as if you are the only person going through this fatherless experience on planet earth? When the word island is mentioned today many individuals think of the old famous television show, Gilligan's Island. If you have never heard of this show before, it was about a group of individuals that were stranded on a deserted island, displaying in a comical format how they survived and their attempts to get off of the island. The following is part of their theme song:

> Just sit right back and you'll hear a tale, a tale of a fateful trip
> That started from this tropic port, aboard this tiny Ship.
> The mate was a mighty sailin' man, the Skipper brave and sure,
> Five passengers set sail that day for a three hour tour.
> A three hour tour.
> The weather started getting rough, the tiny ship was tossed.
> If not for the courage of the fearless crew, the Minnow would be lost.
> The Minnow would be lost...[7]

Though you may feel like Gilligan, all alone on your individual island, you must realize you are never alone. Hebrews 13:5 assures us of this in saying "for He hath said I will never leave thee nor forsake thee." When you feel most alone remember God is near to you!

 ## ACTION - In My Prayer Journal

Make a list of the times you feel most alone. Begin to ask God to give you strength and comfort in those times.

Suggested Prayer: Dear Lord, please help me today to be aware of Your presence. Help me to remember that You are near when I may feel alone, because Your Scriptures say You will never leave me nor forsake me. Amen.

The Fatherless Journey

The Fatherless Journey

Day 6

You Are Loved

"I am crucified with Christ: nevertheless I live; yet not I, but Christ liveth in me: and the life which I now live in the flesh I live by the faith of the Son of God, Who loved me, and gave Himself for me." Galatians 2:20

Do you ever feel unloved? It is common to feel this way when you are fatherless. Growing up I always knew that my mom loved me, but it felt as if I was half loved because there was no fatherly love at times. During special events in my life it would have been nice to have that fatherly love right by my side. One day during my eighth grade year, my English teacher asked me to write a poem for a competition. I always enjoyed writing so I started. At first it was hard, but then God brought a poem to my heart where I could express my inner feelings of fatherlessness. The following is the last four stanzas in that poem:

> Then I realized GOD is on my side,
> He will never leave me and has never lied.
> So my Father now is God above,
> He has been ever since I trusted in His love.

It is true God does love us. He loved us so much that he sent His own Son to die for us. I challenge you today to not forget how much you are loved!

-Paul

CHALLENGE – Day 6

Think to yourself for a moment about what you believe love really is. Many people differ on their opinion of love. For all of us love is a needed act or gift toward us. When we know we are loved our day is better and the sun seems to shine a little brighter. What happens though when we do not feel loved? This is one of the most crucial parts of a fatherless individual's life. Many of the bad statistics resulting from fatherlessness have a direct connection from the lack of love in the child or teen's life. No matter how unloved you may feel at times you should be comforted to know that Christ loves you. He loved you so much that He was crucified on a cross, stabbed in the side with a sword, spat upon, forced to wear a crown of thorns, mocked, and ultimately persecuted for most of his life. He loves us so much that He died for us. Galatians 2:20 tells us that as Christians we are crucified with Christ. Many times our lives will not be easy, but we can rest assured that no matter what problems we will face we have the ability to get through them simply by resting in the love of Christ.

 ACTION - In My Prayer Journal

Write a letter to Jesus thanking Him for what He has done for your life.

Suggested Prayer: Dear Lord, I thank You for dying for me and for giving me hope of eternity in Heaven with You! I love You and thank You for loving me! Amen.

The Fatherless Journey

The Fatherless Journey

Day 7
Consequences for Not Climbing

"Wherefore he saith, Awake thou that sleepest, and arise from the dead, and Christ shall give thee light. See then that ye walk circumspectly, not as fools, but as wise, Redeeming the time, because the days are evil. Wherefore be ye not unwise, but understanding what the will of the Lord is." Ephesians 5:14-17

There are only two more days left of preparation until we begin our trip. I am excited as I am sure you are. As we have been preparing have you had any thoughts about not climbing? I am sure that you have. I know I did. Since the climb is so difficult and there are so many obstacles, at this point, many individuals either postpone the climb for an extended period of time or never make the climb at all. Sadly, most individuals defeated by the fatherless mountain usually do not succeed to their fullest potential for the rest of their life. They try to move on but with several unresolved life issues associated with the fatherless mountain; they fall short in succeeding in many other aspects of life. I personally had several friends that chose to lie down; and be defeated, and today they are facing a multitude of consequences including: addiction, abuse, jail time, bitterness, an unsuccessful life path, teen pregnancy, and much more. The statistics are not a joke and failing to conquer this mountain in your life may lead you to becoming one of them. I want to challenge you as we continue preparing, and then as we finally begin the climb, to not give up because the consequences are too great to bear and they will affect you for the rest of your life.

–Paul

CHALLENGE – Day 7

There is an old saying: "Hindsight sees 20/20," which basically means that if you would have known the consequences or rewards of something you did before you did it, you may have changed your actions. Jonah is a famous Bible character from the Old Testament that ultimately displays the meaning of this old saying. Jonah was told by God that he was to go to Nineveh but due to his hatred towards the people of Nineveh he ran from God and did not climb that mountain that was laid before him. The consequences for Jonah not climbing his mountain were tremendous; he was swallowed by a great fish. He should be in the Guinness Book of World Records for being the only person to ever be inside a great fish's belly and live to tell about it. If Jonah would have had hindsight he would have never tried to run from God. Being inside the great fish's belly and then being thrown up by the great fish was most likely not a glamorous experience. Once Jonah saw that the only option was to serve the Lord he began to walk in God's steps. His life was quickly used by God to reach individuals. Ephesians 5:14-17 shows us that we must redeem the time that God has given to us. We must walk in the Lord's will and He will give us light. At this point in your life God's desire for you is to conquer this mountain. Do not give up for the consequences are too great, and you might get eaten by a great fish!

 ## ACTION - In My Prayer Journal

Make a list of the top 5 things that you know God wants you to do with your life right now. Some examples would be: respecting your parents, climbing this mountain, living a pure life, giving 100% in school, witnessing to a friend, quitting a bad habit, etc.

Suggested Prayer: Dear Lord, only through You and Your strength can I conquer this mountain in my life. Please help me today to seek You and Your strength through any life circumstances that I may face. Amen.

The Fatherless Journey

The Fatherless Journey

Day 8

<u>Overcoming Fear</u>

"For God hath not given us the spirit of fear, but of power, and of love, and of a sound mind." II Timothy 1:7

Growing up I was fearful of a lot of things. I had a fear of the dark, dogs, confrontation, failure, being alone, and much more. I know that they were not all the direct result of being fatherless, but many of my fears stemmed from that situation. I remember living in an old house in my home town. When day turned to night I always feared that someone may break in, and there was no man there to protect us. Now before you laugh, I was only four years old at the time, but the fear was real and continued on throughout much of my childhood. One day in 7th grade I went snow skiing for the first time. Initially I was scared of it as well. When I got to the top of the hill, all I could do was look down at this huge mountain and think in fear how I would ever make it down. I did not know how to control my skis, how to turn from right to left, or how to stop. I was a beginner. After about 2 hours, I made it down the slope for the first time. This mountain was set up differently than most ski resorts, whereas the lodge and parking lot were on the top of the mountain. I was very excited to get on the ski lift and go back to the lodge. As I was getting on the lift, my youth pastor and former mentor decided to ride up with me. Since he was the unlucky individual that had to teach me how to ski that evening, he became very well aware that I was afraid. Knowing of this fear he quoted to me II Timothy 1:7. I think it was the first time I had ever heard this verse or the first time it really caught my attention. Finally, I realized I needed to begin conquering these fears that were inhibiting me for such a long time. I challenge you today to not let any of your fears get in your way, seek God for help in conquering your fears.

–Paul

CHALLENGE – Day 8

September 11, 2001, is a historic day for the United States. Many individuals remember exactly what they were doing when they heard of the events that were taking place. It was a shock to the nation. Many heroes came about from this historic day, due to their efforts in acting in time of need. One such man was named Todd Beamer. Todd boarded Flight United 93 going from Newark, NJ to San Francisco, CA. His flight was on one of the planes that were hijacked that day by terrorists and instead of going to San Francisco as he had planned; his flight was being re-routed to Washington DC. Todd and a few other passengers on the plane knew that they had to do something. They could not just sit in their seats with fear and allow these terrorists to complete their mission. Todd's last audible words were, "Are you guys ready? Let's roll." The group conquered fear and took over the plane which soon came crashing down in a field in Somerset, Pennsylvania. Though none of the passengers on that flight survived that day, Todd became known as a national hero, because he gave his life to save others. They overcame their fear and conquered the obstacles that were set in front of them. [8] II Timothy 1:7 shows us that fear is not from God. Fear limits us from living to our fullest potential. What are you fearful of? II Timothy 1:7 also shows us that God hath given us power, love, and a sound mind. When you become fearful, remember that we have power through the Lord; trust Him today to help you overcome your fear.

 ACTION - In My Prayer Journal

Write out a list of all of your fears. Begin meditating on II Timothy 1:7 daily thinking of your fears, and ask God to help you conquer them.

Suggested Prayer: Dear Lord, I realize only through You am I able to overcome my fears. I ask that from this day forward You will strengthen me to live with power, love, and a sound mind. Amen.

The Fatherless Journey

The Fatherless Journey

Day 9

Dealing with Discouragement

"Cast thy burden upon the LORD, and He shall sustain thee: He shall never suffer the righteous to be moved." Psalm 55:22

Well, we are finally here. Today is the last day of preparation, and tomorrow begins week 1 of our trip. Have you felt any discouragement during preparation, or have you been discouraged about the trip in any way? If you have, it is completely normal. You are trying to conquer one of the hardest obstacles you will ever face in your life. When I was your age, I used to constantly deal with discouragement. Fatherlessness and discouragement go hand in hand. I used to be discouraged about my schoolwork, sports, appearance, abilities, and much more, but I was able to get through it. I finally realized that through God I am sufficient. I challenge you today to deal with your discouragement. The summer before my eleventh grade high school year I went to Canada for a backpacking/canoeing trip with my high school basketball team. The trip was approximately 80 miles and lasted for about 10 days. It was an experience to say the least. When we backpacked on land it was called a portage, because we had to carry our canoes as well. The night before a very long portage (approximately 3.5 miles) the older players on the team thought that they would help the younger players. We decided to take their canoes over that night so that there burdens would not be as difficult the next day. They were only responsible to carry their backpack now instead of a backpack and a canoe over their head. It was not an easy trip for us, but it helped out the junior high players, and they were very grateful. They were glad to cast their burdens on us, and we enjoyed helping them deal with their discouragement. I challenge you today to cast your burdens on the Lord for only He will be able to help you deal with your discouragement!

–Paul

CHALLENGE – Day 9

The yells, sounds of marching, and sounds of chariots were drawing nigh. They were getting very nervous and fearful that they were going to be taken captive again and possibly even murdered. Suddenly, Moses lifted his rod toward the Heavens, trusting that God would save them, and the miracle of the Red Sea parting took place. The waters drew back from side to side providing a pathway to walk free and clear, and as soon as they were all across, the waters came tumbling down destroying the soldiers that sought destruction upon their lives. (Exodus 14). God had delivered them from their discouragement and at the end of this trial the Bible says, "And Israel saw that great work which the LORD did upon the Egyptians: and the people feared the LORD, and believed the LORD, and his servant Moses." Exodus 14:31. This is just one example of the many times Moses cast burdens upon the Lord for himself and the Israelites during their journey through the wilderness to the Promised Land, and He miraculously delivered them. No matter the circumstances they faced, God sustained them! Psalm 55:22 tells us to "Cast our burdens upon the Lord, because He will sustain us." Only God is able to help us in every moment of our life. By allowing God to deal with your discouragement, you too shall be able to look back and see what great things He has done for you. Deal with your discouragement by giving it to God today!

 ## ACTION - In My Prayer Journal

Make a list of the items you are currently discouraged about in your life. Pray over them and then begin praying for 30 days straight that God would deliver you from discouragement.

Suggested Prayer: Dear Lord, I give You my burdens. I ask that in this time of discouragement in my life that You would sustain me. I trust You and love You! Amen.

The Fatherless Journey

THE TRIP - WEEK 1

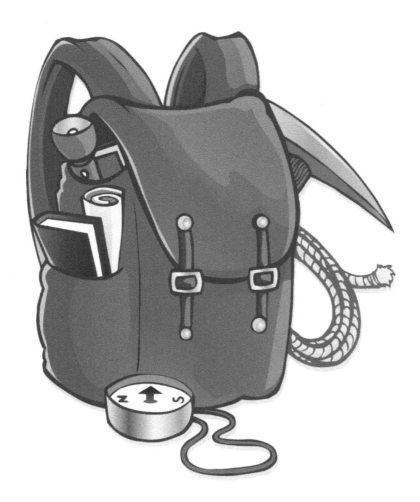

Days 10-16

The Fatherless Journey

Day 10

Forgiveness

"Let all bitterness, and wrath, and anger, and clamour, and evil speaking, be put away from you, with all malice. And be ye kind one to another, tenderhearted, forgiving one another, even as God for Christ's sake hath forgiven you."
Ephesians 4:31-32

When I was 10 months old my father left our home never to return. His leaving, though hard, was actually a blessing in disguise. In addition to his addictions, he was a very angry and abusive man. On several occasions he physically and mentally abused my mother. This makes me tremble in anger just to tell you, because I love her dearly, and I think that any man that abuses a woman is a coward. He never abused me, but one night when I was a few months old, he came home in a drunken rampage and threw my mother, brother, and sister out of our trailer keeping me inside with him. My mother went to a neighbor's house and called the police. When the police arrived they forced my father to give me to them. Instead of gently surrendering to the police he threw me to them. That is right, he threw me! To this day I am thankful that the officer could catch! My life could have ended that night, or I could have been severely hurt if I would have hit the ground. For many years it was hard not to be bitter toward my father for abusing my mother, for abandoning us, and for throwing me to the police, and I even used to think when I was a child, that someday I would visit him and return to him the pain that he caused my family. I can assure you that this never happened, because I forgave him for all that he had done. The results of bitterness and anger are not worth it. I am sure that your story is completely different than mine, but I do know that no matter what your father or anyone else has done to you, you must forgive. I challenge you to forgive those who have caused you anger and let go of any bitterness or grudge that you may have towards them.

-Paul

CHALLENGE – Day 10

You cannot escape the reality that in life there are times when you must forgive people. Since no man is perfect, they are prone to, at times, bring hurt and disappointment. Forgiveness is a major step towards success in every fatherless child's life. You must forgive in order to continue climbing the fatherless mountain. This is the first day of your trip and your most crucial step up the fatherless mountain. You may be thinking to yourself that you have already forgiven your father, and that the step of forgiveness has already been taken in your life. Aside from forgiveness of your father, you may need to forgive others as well. A lot of times there is bitterness and anger stored up that needs released. This bitterness and anger can be directed toward your father, but also toward your mother, siblings, step mother, step dad, someone that has neglected you, someone that you may think caused your father to leave, even anger towards God, or towards someone that I have neglected to mention. When forgiveness is ignored there are always consequences to pay. This consequence could be a broken relationship or a demolished future due to bitterness and anger, a lack of trust in other relationships, and many other things. When bitterness is planted in your life, it brings about growth that is against God. Many times, bitterness causes people to fight, bicker, hate, and even murder. Climbing this first step on your mountain may be the hardest you will take. For some it may involve several steps; meaning that you have more than one person to forgive, but you need to start somewhere.

THE BASIS FOR FORGIVENESS: When Jesus died on the cross for you, He performed the ultimate act of forgiveness. He forgave you for every sin that you have committed and every sin that you will commit in the future. When Christ shed His blood on the cross it was for you to be forgiven of your sins. Just as Christ forgave you, you are responsible to forgive others. You are also responsible to ask forgiveness of any wrong doings that you do to others. There are four steps to this part of the climb up the fatherless mountain:

1. Forgive Your Dad
2. Forgive Yourself
3. Forgive Others, and Ultimately
4. Ask God For Forgiveness.

You must work through these 4 levels of forgiveness as you climb the fatherless mountain, or you will not be able to successfully conquer this struggle in your life.

ACTION - In My Prayer Journal

Make a list of the individuals in your life that you need to forgive. Begin to pray for them and ask God to forgive you for any bitterness, hatred, or anger that you may feel. Then daily seek His strength and guidance to love those that have hurt you.

Suggested Prayer: Dear Lord, please forgive me for not being forgiving to those who have hurt me or who have caused me pain. Please forgive me for my bitterness or anger, and please help me to forgive and love my father, myself, and others and to put You first in my life. Amen.

The Fatherless Journey

The Fatherless Journey
Day 11

Inferiority

"Not that we are sufficient of ourselves to think any thing as of ourselves; but our sufficiency is of God." II Corinthians 3:5

Throughout my childhood, teenage years, college, and even until today, I have often struggled with inferiority. This is a common trait found in most all fatherless individuals. Since we did not have a father for a part of our lives, we have a fair lack of confidence. I used to feel inferior in many things including: sports, academics, performance, individual abilities, appearance, and much more. Many of these inferiorities streamed from fatherlessness. Questions galore, was my mindset as a wondering child, teenager, and young adult without a dad. I always thought to myself how wonderful it would have been to have a father to guide me. I went to a private Christian school and I was among the small percentage that had divorced parents. I would watch my friends with wondrous thoughts roaming through my mind, due to the fact that they had a dad and I did not. They had the opportunity to learn the key essentials about life from a man, and I did not. They had a man to teach them to be a man, and I did not. No matter the home situation, I thought if my friends had a dad, then they had to be luckier than I was! I learned later in life that this in itself was a fallacy. There were many children and teenagers that I knew that physically had a father, but there was still an absence in their life. Inferiority has continued throughout most of my life, throughout my personal life and career. The only way to conquer inferiority is by giving it to God, and realizing that my sufficiency is from Him and Him alone. I challenge you today to remember that God created you who He wanted you to be, and for this very reason no man is better than you.

-Paul

CHALLENGE – Day 11

Another aspect of coming to grips in your fatherless situation is understanding that you do not have someone to call dad or daddy on this earth. A dad is more than just a father. When someone has a dad they have something special. A dad is someone that loves you and cares for every one of your needs and strives to push you toward your greatest potential. A dad is a man that teaches you about the things of life. Dads teach their sons about driving, about girls and dating, and about masculinity. A dad also takes his son camping, hunting, fishing, and even to work with him. A dad is firm, but loving. A dad teaches you how to play sports, how to fight, and how to do other manly things. Since you are fatherless you don't have a dad to teach you these things. Whether your father has passed away or he simply lives down the street from you, there are still feelings of inferiority present. Your friends may tell you about an activity with their dad or about something their dad taught them, and this may make you feel empty and wanting for that type of relationship. This is understandable and normal in your circumstance. Though this feeling may never disappear completely, there are steps that you can take to realize that you are not inferior to anyone. Vince Papale is a perfect example of an individual conquering inferiority. His story was so inspiring that Disney created the movie <u>Invincible</u> after him. Entering the NFL at age 30, Vince was the oldest rookie in NFL history to play without the benefit of college football experience.[9] Regardless of Vince's inferiority, he was determined and became a legacy in the NFL. The same goes with your life, many times your inferiority may be overwhelming, but if you continue to trust God with your inferiority you will be able to live a successful life. II Corinthians 3:5 says "Not that we are sufficient of ourselves to think anything as of ourselves; but our sufficiency is of God."

 ACTION - In My Prayer Journal

Make a list of the items in your life that are lacking because of not having a dad. Then begin to pray daily that God will help you overcome your inferiority.

Suggested Prayer: Dear Lord, I give to You my inferiority; I trust You for You have made me and my sufficiency is from You. I thank You for being my confidence and my strength. Amen.

The Fatherless Journey

The Fatherless Journey

Day 12

<u>Trusting God</u>

"Trust in the LORD with all thine heart; and lean not unto thine own understanding.
In all thy ways acknowledge Him, and He shall direct thy paths." Proverbs 3:5-6

Do you ever struggle with trusting God with certain parts of your life? I have, and when I was your age, I tremendously struggled with trusting Him. I knew I was supposed to, but many times knowing and actually doing were two completely different things. Once I got to the point where I was actively trusting, my life became much easier. Many times fatherless individuals feel that they are in a disconnect with God. Some say this is due to the lack of a manly influence on our lives, and how we view our fathers has a connection with how we view God the Father. This may be true, but it should not stop us from pursuing a close relationship with God, including trusting Him with every day of our lives. I challenge you to give this entire mountain and journey to Him, because only through His guidance, strength, and care are we able to succeed.

-Paul

CHALLENGE – Day 12

Today it seems that more and more sports players are revealing that they have a personal relationship with Jesus Christ. Many will praise God when they win a game or do something spectacular such as score a touchdown, hit a home run, make the final three pointer at the buzzer, or other remarkable events but what about when they miss the shot, lose the game, or even strike out? As fans, we hope that they will still continue to trust God with their losses just as well as their victories. As you climb your fatherless mountain there will be victories and there will be losses. Proverbs 3:5-6 gives us guidance on how we need to trust in every life circumstance. In Daniel 6, we read of how Daniel, though a faithful servant and follower of God, was cast into a lion's den. The intention for this punishment was that he would be eaten and destroyed. Even though he had been following God consistently, God allowed Daniel to go through this trial. Even in the lion's den Daniel trusted God, and this was the result: "My God hath sent his angel, and hath shut the lions' mouths, that they have not hurt me: forasmuch as before him innocency was found in me; and also before thee, O king, have I done no hurt." Daniel 6:22. In the good times and the bad times, trust God with your life for only He can protect you!

 ACTION - In My Prayer Journal

Write out your victories and losses in life from the past month. Then write out how you could better trust God through the losses and better praise Him in the victories.

Suggested Prayer: Dear Heavenly Father, please help me today to trust You with every aspect of my life. You have created me and I trust that You will guide me through any circumstance that I may face. Amen.

The Fatherless Journey

The Fatherless Journey

Day 13

Uncontrolled Anger

"Be ye angry, and sin not: let not the sun go down upon your wrath. Let all bitterness, and wrath, and anger, and clamour, and evil speaking, be put away from you, with all malice." Ephesians 4:26, 31

Many times in my fatherless experience I had uncontrolled anger. My anger was partially due to the lack of male guidance on my temper and partially due to bitterness of being fatherless. I am embarrassed to talk about this now, but in junior and senior high there were times that I would start fights with peers, disrespect authority, yell at my mom and other family members, and other such destructive behavior. I was an angry, bitter young man. One day in youth group our assistant pastor was preaching on anger. He showed us that even just being angry is sin and he challenged us to control our anger. Suddenly the conviction came upon me. I knew that hatred and bitterness were wrong, but now I could not even be angry. From that day forward I began to work on my anger, and my life became much simpler without fighting, yelling, and angry feelings. Now do not get me wrong, I was not perfect, but through God's help, even until today, there has been much change in this area. I challenge you today to strive to be a loving individual despite your situation.

-Paul

CHALLENGE – Day 13

Football is a great sport. It is packed with action, drama, and adventure. Many times games will have viewers on the edge of their seats. In a recent Super Bowl, there were several penalties due to personal fouls that could have cost the game for either team. These personal fouls were the result of uncontrolled anger. The players knew their boundaries and still acted out in a way that resulted in consequences for the entire team. They let their anger control them to the point that they did not care anymore. How about you? Is your anger controlled or uncontrolled? Are you going to continue to be angry over this fatherless situation or let bitterness continue to consume your life? Verses 26 and 31 of Ephesians chapter 4 command us to be not angry, and then states that it is sin, and Ephesians 4:31 commands us to put away anger and bitterness. Uncontrolled anger is displeasing in the site of God. Begin striving today to control your anger; uncontrolled anger usually has devastating results.

 ## ACTION - In My Prayer Journal

Write out the things or people in your life that make you angry. Also write out the things or people that you have bitterness towards. Begin praying about them and work on overcoming anger and bitterness.

Suggested Prayer: Lord, I ask that You will please forgive me for any anger and bitterness in my life. I ask You to please help me to be loving and forgiving this day forward. Only through You and Your power will I be able to do so. Amen.

The Fatherless Journey

The Fatherless Journey

Day 14
Fearfully & Wonderfully Made

"For Thou hast possessed my reins: Thou hast covered me in my mother's womb. I will praise Thee; for I am fearfully and wonderfully made: marvellous are Thy works; and that my soul knoweth right well." Psalm 139:13-14

Isn't this verse amazing? Just when you begin to wonder if you are special or why you were ever even born, this verse is cast right before your eyes. I was always encouraged to know that despite my circumstances and my shortcomings in being fatherless, the Scriptures consistently showed me that I am fearfully and wonderfully made. When I was growing up, I always had doubt about myself in many aspects of my life. Whether it was sports, my appearance, work, or whatever else, I had doubt or fear that I was not good at it and never was going to be good at it. After finding this verse I was very excited to know that God created me to be exactly what he wanted me to be. I am God's blessed creation and no one, no rude comment, or anything else can change that. God made us; he gave us hands to work, ears to hear, eyes to see, legs to walk, a mouth to talk, and all of the other attributes of our lives. By His ability, everything was put together in a fearfully and wonderfully made creation. I challenge you today to trust God despite your downfalls or shortcomings, and remember He made you, and you are who He wanted you to be!

-Paul

CHALLENGE – Day 14

You were fearfully and wonderfully made (Psalm 139:13-14). That is correct; this verse is referring to you! You were fearfully and wonderfully made. Despite your personal criticism toward yourself and others' criticism of you, you are God's blessed creation. Despite your circumstances God made you who He wanted you to be! God has allowed this situation to occur in your life. God made you with the ability to get through this fatherless journey. TLC or The Learning Channel is comprised of several television programs. Many of these programs feature individuals with unique life situations that range from little people, to big people, to families with multiple children, or to people that are in need of some type of help. Imagine if they would develop a TV show that presented a different fatherless child or teen each week, it would be intriguing to see how each fatherless individual's situation is completely different. Displayed would be several similar circumstances such as hurt, pain, frustration, and inferiority. Despite what good or bad elements viewers would see by watching a documentary on your life, the true fact is fearfully and wonderfully made is your design by the designer God Himself. In His eyes you are a masterpiece worth more than money can buy. Always remember to praise the Lord for creating you who you are!

 ## ACTION - In My Prayer Journal

Write out the picture viewers would see if they watched your television show. Be honest. If there are items that you are not satisfied with, handle them as you can, and then give the rest to God. Try to daily improve your TV show as you continue conquering the fatherless mountain!

Suggested Prayer: Dear Lord, please help me to realize and remember that I am who You made me to be. If there are items in my life that I need to change, please reveal them to me and guide me to change. For the things that I cannot change due to my circumstances, please help me to remember that I am fearfully and wonderfully made. Amen.

The Fatherless Journey

The Fatherless Journey

Day 15

Self Esteem

"Let no man despise thy youth; but be thou an example of the believers, in word, in conversation, in charity, in spirit, in faith, in purity." I Timothy 4:12

As I picked up my duffle bag and began to walk across the field after a soccer game, something seemed to be missing. This same feeling happened on several occasions and in several different scenarios. The ending of events such as sports games, school plays, award ceremonies, and other similar events were often difficult because of my situation. I would see my friends being greeted by their fathers. Now do not get me wrong, my mother was always there, and I can say that I am truly grateful for that, but when one parent is missing, it is as if you are off balance. The mother and the father have completely different roles to play, and they are not capable of filling the void of the other for us. This imbalance often produces an image of low self-esteem which I had and many other fatherless individuals face. We must fill this void through God, realizing we cannot fix the situation, but seek the Lord for His strength. I challenge you today to get your self-esteem from God and not from your own feelings.

-Paul

CHALLENGE – Day 15

Michael Jordan is undoubtedly the greatest basketball player ever to play in the NBA. He set records and accomplished such a variety of things that current NBA players only dream of. It appears that his life has always been this way, but this is not the case. When Michael was a Sophomore in high school he was not considered anywhere near the best. He tried out for the varsity basketball team during his sophomore year, but at 5'11" he was deemed too short to play at that level and was cut from the team. This cut most likely led to a season of low self-esteem in his life, but the following summer, however, he grew four inches and trained rigorously. His junior year of high school he earned a position on the varsity roster averaging about 20 points per game. Michael may have had low self-esteem at a point in his life, but after practice and persistence, he became one of the most confident people to play a professional sport. [10] What about you? Your fatherless circumstances may lead you to low self-esteem at times. There are things in your life where you may feel insufficient. One thing you can have confidence in is your Christian walk. I Timothy 4:12 "Let no man despise thy youth; but be thou an example of the believers, in word, in conversation, in charity, in spirit, in faith, in purity." Your self-esteem should come from God and God alone.

 ACTION - In My Prayer Journal

Make a list of the positions you could be in: where you could be an example to your peers. Begin praying for these items, and ask God to help you be an example with high self-esteem.

Suggested Prayer: Dear Lord, help me to remember that I am sufficient through You. Help me to be an example to my peers, family, and friends. Only through Your guidance and strength am I able. Amen.

The Fatherless Journey

The Fatherless Journey

Day 16

Give Your Life To God

"For none of us liveth to himself, and no man dieth to himself. For whether we live, we live unto the Lord; and whether we die, we die unto the Lord: whether we live therefore, or die, we are the Lord's. For to this end Christ both died, and rose, and revived, that He might be Lord both of the dead and living." Romans 14:7-9

Hello my friend, can you believe that today is the end of week 1? This trip has been exciting to see the progress that you have made on your fatherless journey. I am glad that you allowed me to come with you. I am proud of you, especially since you have not given up. Today we will conquer the last part of the incline. It will not be an easy one, but it is essential to moving on to week 2. When I was 15 years old, I went with my youth group to a youth conference in North Carolina. The Conference was fun. We went to an amusement park and a rodeo, stayed in a hotel for a week, and much more. Most of what I remember from that week was that we had to sit and listen to a lot of preaching from some solid men of God. Now do not get me wrong, I was a typical goof-off teenager, but for some reason, the speakers drew my attention that week. In one of the services I went forward and gave my life to God: surrendering to full time Christian service. I have had friends that have given their lives to God, and they have chosen a variety of different career paths: doctors, lawyers, policemen, builders, and many other great occupations. No matter what career we choose, we must still give our life to God and follow His perfect will for our lives. You may not know your future occupation today, but you do need to give your life to God, realizing that it is His already. He is the Creator, the Father, and the Savior. I challenge you today to give every aspect of your life to God.

-Paul

CHALLENGE – Day 16

On day 1 you were presented with Salvation and giving your heart to Jesus. Day 12 you learned about trusting God, and today is giving your life to God. In Romans 14:7-9 it says that "We are the Lord's." If you surrender to His perfect will for your life, it will be a lot easier than if you tried to go on your own life path. In Revelations 3:15-16 it says: "I know thy works, that thou art neither cold nor hot: I would thou wert cold or hot. So then because thou art lukewarm, and neither cold nor hot, I will spue thee out of my mouth." These two verses show that we as humans are either for Christ (hot) or against Christ (cold). It is better for us to be upfront about being cold or hot than to be partially for Christ and partially for the world (lukewarm). As Christians we must be on fire for Christ, there is no room nor is there any time for us to be lukewarm, and there is a punishment for this type of behavior. Being a lukewarm Christian makes Christ want to vomit. Now you have three choices that you have to pick from in your life: do you want to be cold and reject Christ, do you want to be lukewarm and make Christ vomit, or do you want to be hot and serve Christ in every area of your life? There are a multitude of examples in the Bible, throughout history, and even around you today where individuals either gave their life to God or they did not, and you and I get to learn from their examples. A famous preacher named Adrian Rogers once said, "He must be Lord of all to be Lord at all." Give your life to God today, and surrender to his ultimate plan for your life.

 ## ACTION - In My Prayer Journal

Write out a letter to God telling Him the things in your life that you need and want to surrender to Him. Pray for those things that you have a hard time letting go of. Tell Him you give Him your life and really mean it.

Suggested Prayer: Dear Lord, I realize that in order for You to be Lord at all, You need to be Lord of all areas of my life. You are my Master and Creator, and I give You every aspect of my life today. Thank You for constantly giving me guidance on this journey and I ask for Your strength for the next two weeks.

The Fatherless Journey

THE TRIP - WEEK 2

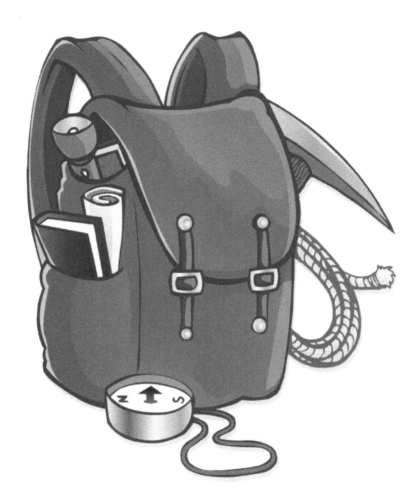

Days 17-23

The Fatherless Journey

Day 17

<u>Submission To Authority</u>

"Children, obey your parents in the Lord: for this is right. Honour thy father and mother; which is the first commandment with promise; That it may be well with thee, and thou mayest live long on the earth." Ephesians 6:1-3

"Let every soul be subject unto the higher powers. For there is no power but of God: the powers that be are ordained of God. Whosoever therefore resisteth the power, resisteth the ordinance of God: and they that resist shall receive to themselves damnation. For rulers are not a terror to good works, but to the evil. Wilt thou then not be afraid of the power? do that which is good, and thou shalt have praise of the same." Romans 13:1-3

Throughout childhood, teenage years, college, and even until today, I have struggled with submitting to the authority that was put into my life. Whether it was a teacher, preacher, boss, coach, aunt, uncle, parent, or whomever, it has always been hard to submit to them. As I have gotten older, and as I have matured as a Christian, it has become easier. I can honestly say that very rarely do I struggle with submission today, but it has been a growing process. When you do not have a father in your life to teach you about submission, often it is hard to learn. Some individuals are blessed with mothers who have this keen ability to force their children into submission, but many of us had mothers that tried but were just good at being a mother. I have found that the more I submit to my authority, the easier it makes my life and my authority's life; and more importantly it honors God. I challenge you today to submit to the authority that God has placed in your life. Remember, it pleases God when we honor individuals that He has placed over us.

-Paul

CHALLENGE – Day 17

Authority is everywhere, regardless of your age; you will always have authority over you. Authority ranges from parents to bosses and from teachers to other adults in your life. Authority is the government, the law, and anyone placed over you in any regard. Even when you step onto an airplane for a flight, you are under the authority of the flight attendant and the flight attendant is under the authority of the pilot. Typically, authority has experience that you do not possess. A man named Bill is in the United States Navy. He serves his country with dignity and honor. His service involves a multitude of duties. He is responsible to fulfill his designated job; plus, he is required to keep himself and his belongings in tip-top shape. He has to report to an officer directly above him. If one day Bill decided not to do his chores, and not to listen to his authority, there would be very large consequences to pay. He is required to live according to the standards of the United State Navy. What about you? Being a Christian, you are in the army of God. You are a Christian soldier. Part of this amazing privilege is that you must submit to the authority that is over you. On your fatherless journey strive to submit to the authority that is in your life. Romans 13:1 "Let every soul be subject unto the higher powers."

 ACTION - In My Prayer Journal

Write out the authority figures that are currently in your life. Then put an <u>R</u> beside the names that you feel you have respected or who you currently respect, and then put a <u>D</u> beside those names you have been disrespectful to. Work on trying to have all <u>R</u>'s within the next 30 days, despite how hard it may seem.

Suggested Prayer: Dear Lord, I ask for Your forgiveness for the disrespect that I have shown in the past, and I seek Your strength to respect and submit to the authority that You have placed and will place in my life. Amen.

The Fatherless Journey

The Fatherless Journey

Day 18

Man of God

"Nevertheless the foundation of God standeth sure, having this seal, The Lord knoweth them that are His. And, Let everyone that nameth the name of Christ depart from iniquity." II Timothy 2:19

Being fatherless, I grew up with the option to decide who I wanted to be. I could be a movie star, sports player, teacher, boss, or a multitude of different people. While I climbed up the fatherless mountain, I soon realized that most everyone that did not have a relationship with Christ were living empty lives. They were famous or successful for some earthly reason, but true happiness and meaning were absent. The true heroes in my life became the Godly men and women around me. They were heroes because they were leading by example and showing me how to be a man of God. A few traits that I have found to be common amongst men of God are: patience, kindness, love, tenderheartedness, boldness in Christ, constant in prayer, slow to anger, God fearing, pure, consistent, and forgiving. I am not saying you have to have these characteristics overnight, but they are something to work towards. We will never be perfect on this earth, but life is filled with hope and joy when we attempt to be true men of God. I challenge you today to strive to be a man of God.

-Paul

CHALLENGE – Day 18

Have you ever read the book of Job or heard his story in church or in a Sunday School Class? Often it is easy for our imaginations to group Biblical individuals as "Bible Characters" just as Mickey Mouse or Bugs Bunny are "Disney Characters". It may be because we refer to them as "characters" or it may be that we consider them to be cartoons instead of once living. Job was a real person just like you; he was not a fictional character in any way, but a true, real man of God. His story is amazing and many of us could not even begin to imagine going through what he did in such a short time (The Book of Job). He lost his children, health, wealth, and dignity all in a matter of hours. Despite it all, he was still a man of God. Despite his own wife telling him to curse God and die, he was still a man of God. He knew that God had allowed these things to happen for a reason. Just like Job, strive to be a man of God, despite anything that you may be facing in your life.

 ACTION - In My Prayer Journal

Write out anything that comes between you and God. Examples would be possessions, friends, sin, entertainment, or a variety of other things. Pray that God would help you to overcome these things and that He will help you to grow daily as a man of God.

Suggested Prayer: Dear Lord, help me today to live for You. Give me strength to resist temptation and to follow You despite what challenges may come into my life. I want to be a man of God today and the rest of my life. Amen.

The Fatherless Journey

The Fatherless Journey

Day 19

Man of the House

"Brethren, let every man, wherein he is called, therein abide with God."
I Corinthians 7:24

Being the man of the house is a very life-changing role that you have been faced with. Whether you are an only child or have other siblings, you have a very crucial role in being the man of the house or one of the men of the house. September 1, several years ago, I officially became the sole man of my house. Up to the day he died, my grandfather held the position. The day that he passed is as clear as if it happened just yesterday. Aside from the hurt and pain of his death, I remember thinking to myself "who will lead." Surely not the boy who just turned 12, how could I be forced into this position? Although you are not the authority in your household at this point, you do have a load of responsibility heaped upon you. Since at this point it was just me and my grandmother, I realized that I had new obligations. Soon after September 1, I had to begin to grow up fast. If something broke, I had to fix it or figure out how to get it fixed. If work needed done such as yard work, snow shoveling, home improvements, or anything else, I had to do it. I took it as my responsibility. Certainly there were times when I did not feel like doing tasks, but I would soon come to realize if I did not do these things no one else would. I remember looking at the tools that had been left to me by my grandfather and realizing they were now mine to use. Becoming the man of the house was not easy, but God got me through it. He gave me the strength and guidance to accomplish these new tasks that had been laid in front of me. I challenge you today to trust God to guide you to lead your house.

-Paul

CHALLENGE – Day 19

Does Paul's situation sound similar to your circumstances? It may be identical or it may be just a glimpse. Regardless, you or you along with your brothers are now the men of the house. This is a huge responsibility and it should not be taken lightly. You may be reading this and be in an orphanage or children's home. If this is the case, help to lead wherever you live. There will always be opportunities where you may be able to help out. There was once a youth pastor that had been given a monumental task. His father-in-law was the senior pastor of his church, and it was discovered that he had ran off with another woman leaving this young youth pastor with a devastated congregation and a church with debt problems. This youth pastor was instantly left in charge as the new senior pastor. Not only did he have to pick up the pieces, but it was caused by his own father-in-law. He began to pray and work hard to repair the damage that his father-in-law had left. It took several years, but today he is still the senior pastor, serving God with all his heart at the church, which eventually became debt free. He could not have taken over and been as successful as he was without relying on God. What about you? You can either overlook the problems of your house and not help out, or you can do what is honoring and pleasing to God and do your best to be the man of the house. From this day forward act as I Corinthians 7:24 tells us to act: "Brethren, let every man, wherein he is called, therein abide with God." Through God you can pick up the pieces of what your father may have left behind.

 ## ACTION - In My Prayer Journal

Write out the responsibilities that you have been given due to being fatherless. Pray about them daily. If there are things you do not know how to do either research it on the internet or ask a male figure in your church, school, or family to show you. You will never learn if you do not ask.

Suggested Prayer: Dear Lord, help me today with my new responsibilities as the man of the house. I haven't asked for these new tasks, but I realize it is my job to do my part. Please give me the strength and wisdom to accomplish these new obstacles to the best of my ability. Please provide someone to teach me the things I do not already know.

The Fatherless Journey

The Fatherless Journey

Day 20

Women

"Now concerning the things whereof ye wrote unto me: It is good for a man not to touch a woman." I Corinthians 7:1

"Ye have heard that it was said by them of old time, Thou Shalt Not Commit Adultery: But I say unto you, That whosoever looketh on a woman to lust after her hath committed adultery with her already in his heart." Matthew 5:27-28

My wife and I had the privilege to date for most of the time from junior high through college. She was the girl of my dreams, and I finally was able to convince her to marry me! Growing up, my wife and I had two completely different home situations, and we joke about it today. She was the pure innocent pastor's daughter that grew up in a solid Biblical family, and I was the bad fatherless bus kid. I am thankful that her parents gave me a chance, but from the beginning, they were very straight-forward with me. They had worked very hard to raise their daughter, and they did not want some guy coming into their home to mess it up. I can honestly say it was not an easy road, but it was worth it. All her parents wanted was for us to be pure. They taught me to treat their daughter with respect. They also taught me that she was God's property and not mine, along with a multitude of other life lessons. The women of my household helped solidify this lesson by teaching me how to behave appropriately with the ladies, and also by teaching me how to be a man that women would desire. To become this kind of man, it does not take any formal training, but an understanding and practice of some certain points and boundaries. I challenge you today to practice the points and boundaries that you will find in today's challenge before you interact with the young lady that you like.

-Paul

CHALLENGE – Day 20

Generally speaking, being a fatherless young man sometimes gives you an advantage in the area of understanding women. Growing up you may be living with your sister, mother, or grandmother. This definitely will give you an advantage in understanding women better than many of your friends. Of course, the ideal situation would be for you to experience and watch how a healthy couple, such as a mother and father relate and interact with one another, but you have to accept what you have been given. God will bring couples into your life that will be examples for you, and you can pick the pieces out of each of their relationships that you think classify how a woman should be treated. Many times this will make you a romanticist. If you have a sister, be there for her, help her when she needs it, protect her and love her, despite how hard it may be. If you live with your mother or grandmother, respect her, show her love, and take care of her. Most likely she is hurting inside or struggling with some issues, and the last thing you should do is add to her pain. It has been found that the way you treat your mother or sister is the same way you will treat your wife. When the time comes for you to find that special girl, treat her with the utmost respect, and abstain from physical affection with her. Respect her parents' wishes. Love her and remember she belongs to God and not you. Whoever God brings into your life, follow the Scriptures' guidance, especially in I Corinthians 7:1 and Matthew 5:27-28. Remember that you do not necessarily need to have a manly influence to know how to treat or respect women; just remember to follow what the Bible commands. A few qualities of a Godly man in regards to treating women would include but are not limited to the following:

1. **Put God first** – God should always be the first priority in your life.
2. **Respect her** – She is not your possession, she belongs to God, and it is your responsibility to take care of her.
3. **Pray** – Pray daily for the woman that God will have you marry.
4. **Read the Bible** – Seek God's will through His Scriptures.
5. **Don't rush anything** – "It is good for a man not to touch a woman."

ACTION - In My Prayer Journal

Write out a description of your ideal wife. Remember to include her desire to serve God, her appearance, her mindsets, her abilities, her strengths, her personality traits, and whatever else that may come to your mind that eflects a woman of God. Begin praying daily for this woman, asking God to prepare both you and her for your lives together.

Suggested Prayer: Dear Lord, please help me to be a man that is honoring and pleasing to You. Help me to respect my mother and other authority figures. Help me to lead my sister(s) and family. Please guide me to the woman that You will ave me to marry, and prepare us for each other. Only through You am I able to find the woman that You want me to have. Amen.

The Fatherless Journey

The Fatherless Journey

Day 21

<u>Being the Leader</u>

"But let every man prove his own work, and then shall he have rejoicing in himself alone, and not in another." Galatians 6:4

Seventh grade was probably one of the hardest years I have ever faced. It was just after my grandfather, who was my father figure, died and I was learning a lot about other things in life. I was a wreck. I tried so hard to be cool, and I was considered cool by all of the bad kids. I was truly a leader for the bad. I did not respect authority in most circumstances. One of my teachers used to say the following statement to me, "You don't care, and you don't care that you don't care, and that is apathy, and apathy is sin." He was right; I did not care. Another one of my teachers used to kick me out of his class on an almost daily basis and send me to the senior pastor's office. I had a bad mouth and I was a horrible influence to those around me. I am not proud of this part of my life, but I tell you these things, because God eventually changed me. The summer after seventh grade I went to The Wilds youth camp where I made assurance of my salvation. From that day forward I had to strive to prove myself a changed man. For much of the time I was labeled the bad kid, and now I was going to try to be good. It was not easy, and I cannot say I was perfect, but I did try. In fact, in the middle of my eighth grade year my principal took up an offering from the teachers and took me out and bought me a suit, because he saw evidence that I was striving to prove my own work. I challenge you today to be a good leader and not a bad leader, proving your own work as a Christian.

-Paul

CHALLENGE – Day 21

In many fatherless homes, the sons are often responsible to take the place of the leader. Even though this may not be your exact situation, there are areas where you are now required to lead. Whether it be protecting your mother or siblings or something completely different. As Christians we are required to be leaders. To many individuals we may be the only Bible that they will ever read. We are to be leaders of good and of things that are pure. We are to always be strong and to display strong faith. Hebrews 11 is often called the "faith hall of fame" and refers to names such as Abel, Enoch, Noah, Abraham, Jacob, Joseph, and Moses, to name a few. These individuals displayed leadership and a strong faith in God at some point in their lives. They trusted God despite most of the bad circumstances that they may have faced. Good leadership and strong faith in God go hand in hand just as bad leadership and living for sin do. You need to decide today whether you will be a good leader or a bad leader. Do you want to be in the faith hall of fame or the hall of shame; it is your decision. Being a bad leader may be fun for a season, but nothing compares to serving God and living for Him! Galatians 6:4 tells us "But let every man prove his own work." What work have you done and will you prove it? Heavenly accomplishments are the only ones that matter.

 ACTION - In My Prayer Journal

Make a list of the items in your life that you currently lead. Pray for the list and pray for the things that you will lead in the future.

Suggested Prayer: Dear Lord, please help me to become the leader that You would have me to be. Help me to prove my own work with the life You have entrusted me with. Amen.

The Fatherless Journey

The Fatherless Journey

Day 22

Learning By Example

"Every man's work shall be made manifest: for the day shall declare it, because it shall be revealed by fire; and the fire shall try every man's work of what sort it is. If any man's work abide which he hath built thereupon, he shall receive a reward. If any man's work shall be burned, he shall suffer loss: but he himself shall be saved; yet so as by fire. Know ye not that ye are the temple of God, and that the Spirit of God dwelleth in you? If any man defile the temple of God, him shall God destroy; for the temple of God is holy, which temple ye are." I Corinthians 3:13-17

My dad abandoned me and my family when I was 10 months old. I was the youngest of three with a 7 year old brother and a 2 year old sister. Over 14 years had gone by since he had departed from our home, and it was time to meet this man that I called my "birth dad." We traveled to Las Vegas, NV which was, and still is, his city of dwelling. This was not the only reason we went there, since my brother had moved there about 5 years prior to our visit. The time finally came and we landed in Las Vegas. The night of our second day in Las Vegas, I met my father. By this point in my life I was 15 years old 5'11 and 190lbs. My sister was 17 and my brother was 21. Just before I met my father, I was curious as to how he would react. This meeting was not an usual father/son reconciliation. I met my father for the first time in Las Vegas in the front of an Adult Video store where he was employed. As you can probably guess, my dad was, and is, deeply involved in pornography. As I walked closer to him, his appearance gave insight that he was fearful to meet the children that he had abandoned. His eyes were blood shot and his hands were shaking. On one hand, my feelings toward this reunion were of utter confusion; on the other hand, I possessed a satisfied feeling as my father's identity was finally being revealed to me after so many years. Even though my father was nervous to meet us he continued to blame everyone else and everything else for his problems. He was an addict and an abuser. At that moment in my life, I had to make a decision that I have refreshed in my mind several times since that meeting - I would learn from his example. My father was, and still is, an alcoholic, abuser, deceiver, and an addicted miserable man. I have tried on several occasions to build a relationship with him, but it is evident that he does not want to. I am not bitter toward him and I do not hate him, but I have learned from his example. It has not always been easy, but I can honestly say that I am striving not to turn out like my father, not out of vengeance or bitterness, but out of realization that far too many men such as you and I end up like our fathers. I challenge you today to learn from your parents' mistakes without bitterness as your motive, but with a motive of striving to learn and ultimately live for God.

-Paul

CHALLENGE – Day 22

For many, history is not a favorite subject in high school, sad but true. The older individuals are the more interesting history seems to become. It is filled with real life stories of war, love, peace, happiness, tragedy, and much more. Parts of history are used as examples in sermons, speeches, and presentations to clarify a specific point or topic. Many of the most popular films in Hollywood are drawn from historical events. One of the most important aspects of history is that it is a resource for all individuals to learn from examples. You can find consequences, trials, and adversity that were developed from the actions of historians. This allows us to change our methods on how we may deal with something today. Even the President of the United States may look at historical situations before he reacts to a current event, because the saying is true, "hind sight sees 20/20." I Corinthians 3:13-17 shows us that we as individuals solely answer for ourselves in God's eyes. Despite what our fathers do or have done, it is our responsibility to manage our lives according to God's will!

 ## ACTION - In My Prayer Journal

Write out certain bad and good characteristics about your father or other manly examples in your life. Begin praying that God will help you become the man that He wants you to be, excluding the bad things that your father or other examples may model.

Suggested Prayer: Dear Lord, I pray that You will help me today to model my life after Your will. I thank You for giving me the opportunity and time to learn from examples of good and bad. Please help me to find some good examples in my life, from history, or in the Bible that I may model my life after. Amen.

The Fatherless Journey

The Fatherless Journey

Day 23

Manhood Without Guidance

"Many are the afflictions of the righteous: but the LORD delivereth him out of them all." Psalm 34:19

Shaving, driving, dating, hunting, dressing, and the list keeps going. Dads are given such a huge responsibility when they have a son. When the dad is not around, who will teach you these things plus the many other life experiences that you are destined to face? Personally, I learned to shave on my own; I learned about cars from my grandfather, my friend Rob, and my father figure Jim. My grandmother taught me to drive; I learned to tie a tie from paper instructions from Sears; I learned how to treat a woman by watching men of God interact with their wives. I was taught to hunt by a friend named Brian and my mentor named Jim; plus, I learned several other important life principles from people by either them teaching me or by my just watching and copying them. I learned many things, especially good work ethic from my mentor, and I learned many key character traits from my father-in-law. Manhood without guidance was not easy, but I got through it and so will you. I am still learning things even today. Do not worry about who will teach you the parts of manhood because God will guide you through it. I challenge you today to let Him guide and develop you into manhood.

-Paul

CHALLENGE – Day 23

Joseph was a great follower of God, but you may not have realized that he was also fatherless for a time in his life. After his brothers had thrown him into the pit and sold him into slavery, he instantly became fatherless. There was no way he could escape and return to his home, and as far as his father knew, he was dead. Joseph was at a crucial time in his young life, when he needed his dad to teach and help him. Despite his circumstances he became a man without guidance. God molded him into the man he wanted him to be, and eventually he was able to prepare a nation for a famine. He and his father did reunite later in life, but during the time of absence Joseph still managed to become a man. You too can be like Joseph. Although it is God's design and his ultimate will for you to be taught by your earthly father, He still will provide the people and wisdom to mold you into the man He wants you to become, if you follow him. Psalm 34:19 "Many are the afflictions of the righteous: but the LORD delivereth him out of them all." Today start trusting God to mold you into the man that he wants you to become.

 ## ACTION - In My Prayer Journal

Make a list of 5 things that you wish you could have learned from your dad. Then begin to pray for them and that God would provide someone or some situation where you could learn them.

Suggested Prayer: Dear Lord, I am a man that is trying to learn without guidance, and I ask that You would guide and teach me to become the man that You want me to be. Only through Your strength and guidance am I able to become a man of You. Amen.

The Fatherless Journey

THE TRIP - WEEK 3

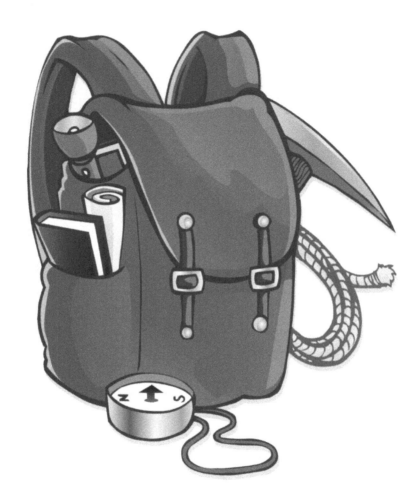

Days 24-30

The Fatherless Journey

Day 24

<u>Be Confident</u>

"And lest I should be exalted above measure through the abundance of the revelations, there was given to me a thorn in the flesh, the messenger of Satan to buffet me, lest I should be exalted above measure. For this thing I besought the Lord thrice, that it might depart from me. And He said unto me, My grace is sufficient for thee: for my strength is made perfect in weakness. Most gladly therefore will I rather glory in my infirmities, that the power of Christ may rest upon me. Therefore I take pleasure in infirmities, in reproaches, in necessities, in persecutions, in distresses for Christ's sake: for when I am weak, then am I strong." II Corinthians 12:7-10

Do you ever doubt yourself? Do you have times when you are not nearly as confident as others? I know I do. Especially when I am trying to do something I have never done before or when I am trying to do something that was very important. When I was in high school I took a night school class to become a beginner electrician. The class was filled with men much older than me. I was there because my mentor thought it would be a good thing for me to learn, especially since I worked with electricity in his company. Since the men in the class were much older than me, I did not have much confidence. Aside from the age difference, I do not know exactly why I was not confident, but this was not the first time that doubt and fear have stopped me from doing things. One day I suddenly realized that I have no reason to doubt or fear. I have the ability to do anything and conquer anything that I partake in while on earth. My favorite verse has always been Philippians 4:13 "I can do all things through Christ which strengtheneth me." Despite my doubt and fear I was able to learn the concepts of the class, but if I would have had confidence all throughout the course, it may have been more effective. I challenge you today to not let the doubt and fear that comes with your fatherless situation keep you from being confident in every aspect of your life. Today give this entire journey to the Lord.

-Paul

CHALLENGE – Day 24

Abraham Lincoln was a great man. Not only was he a great president, but he also is given credit for the abolition of slavery in the United States. Despite his great accomplishments and prestigious positions, honest Abe was not always a success. In fact, he had run for the United States Senate on two occasions and did not win. At this time in his life, he was probably feeling defeated and he probably had a lack of confidence. Despite all of the great things he accomplished later in life, these losses were probably very discouraging. Despite his failures he remained confident, though it was probably not easy, and eventually became the President of the United States. [11] Sometimes you may feel overwhelmed and not have any confidence at all, but there is hope. Luke 1:37 shows us that "For with God nothing shall be impossible." God created this earth. He created it and is the master of everything. He is our Guide, our Deliverer, and our Strength. He sent His Son to die for our sins on the cross to save us from an eternity in Hell. He is Almighty and All Powerful. Be confident in the Lord, for His Grace is sufficient. Trust God today and let him alone be your confidence.

 ## ACTION - In My Prayer Journal

Make a list of the top 10 things in your life that seem to be impossible. Begin praying for these things daily until they are no longer impossible.

Suggested Prayer: Dear Lord, I put my trust in You; please, help me to be confident in You in the good and the bad times. I trust You with my life, and only through You am I able to move forward each day. Amen.

The Fatherless Journey

The Fatherless Journey
Day 25

Mentors – Part I

"For the LORD God is a sun and shield: the LORD will give grace and glory: no good thing will He withhold from them that walk uprightly." Psalm 84:11

I have thought often of what it would have been like if my birth dad would never have left. I wonder where I would be if he would have been the masculine influence in my upbringing. Since my father struggles with several different addictions and was very abusive verbally and physically, it would have hindered my ability to grow up as good as I did. I am not saying that I am perfect, but if I would have had his influence on my life I may be addicted, abused, and even abusive myself. In addition, if you are in a home where your father is physically present but a very poor example to you, please understand that you do not have to turn out like him. I am truly grateful that God did not allow this to happen, but instead He brought men into my life to be my mentors. Although nothing compares to actually having a father of your own, there is a lot that can be learned by having a mentor. During my childhood years, my grandfather was the mentor in my life. He taught me as much as he could while I was a child. He taught me a lot of values that I hold true in my life even to this day. As I mentioned to you previously, my grandfather died when I was in 6th grade. When this happened I was at a very crucial time in my life. The questions were amazing. What about puberty, driving, money, etc.; who would teach me these things? Soon after his death God began to fill the void of a mentor in my life. Although God had taken my grandfather away to be with Him, He provided "replacements" for him. Instead of replacing my grandfather with one mentor he gave me multiple mentors to fill the voids in my life. The names of these men are the following: Jim, Dave, Kerry, Rob, Bryan, Michael, and a few others. Though these names mean absolutely nothing to you; they have influenced my life in more ways than I can remember. My life is truly indebted to these men for the lessons learned and the acts of kindness that they placed upon me. I challenge you to begin looking for a mentor today.

-Paul

CHALLENGE – Day 25

Even though you are fatherless, in every situation there is always a positive element that needs to be addressed: mentors. One of the most interesting parts of being fatherless is that you get to have mentors. What truly is a mentor? A definition of a good mentor would be the following: A Godly male influence that one is able to watch, imitate, and gain knowledge from, in a positive manner, filling the void of being a fatherless child or teenager. A mentor helps the child grow in the right path of life, whether directly or indirectly. Let me tell you about a boy named George, who was eleven years old when his father died. This man George is someone that everyone has heard of. He accomplished great things in his lifetime. This boy later became known as the Father of the United States of America: George Washington. Everyone has seen this great man's face on both a quarter and a one dollar bill. Despite the fatherless mountain in George Washington's life, he had great success. One of the keys to George Washington's success was that he had a mentor in his life. After his father died, his older half-brother became a hero and mentor to him. [12] Just like George Washington, you too need to seek for a mentor in your life. Men that grow up with a father in their home, tend to follow a lot of the examples portrayed by that father. Whether they are good or bad, there is always a comparative process that takes place. In your position this is not the case. You get to have mentors. Pray today, asking God that He may provide a mentor for you.

 ACTION - In My Prayer Journal

Make a list of the characteristics that you would look for in a mentor. For example you may want a man that will teach you how to hunt or how to fix a car. Begin praying that God will provide a Christian mentor that you can model your life after.

Suggested Prayer: Dear Lord, I ask that You will bring into my life a mentor that will teach me life lessons that I have not yet learned, and that will challenge me to live a life that is honoring and pleasing to You. Amen.

The Fatherless Journey

The Fatherless Journey
Day 26

Mentors – Part II

"Pure religion and undefiled before God and the Father is this, To visit the fatherless and widows in their affliction, and to keep himself unspotted from the world." James 1:27

It was a spring Sunday afternoon when I was going out to dinner with my girlfriend and her parents after church. I was 15 years old and just in the middle of my fatherless journey. As we got to the restaurant, we met up with some friends of my girlfriend's family. They seemed to be very nice people. They began to ask me questions about myself during lunch. After a short while, I asked them a question that would alter my future in more ways than I can understand even to this day. I said, "Do you have any work I could do for you around your house?" I was always looking for a way to make an extra buck through physical labor. The woman looked at me and asked if I shoveled snow, and as always, I said yes. From then on I began working at their home doing odd & end jobs. Soon I began working at her husband's business. After a short time, my girlfriend and I had broken up, but my relationship with this family continued on. It has been years since I first met these people and to this day I can say that we are still close. This couple, Jim and Deb, have been examples, guides, and helps for me and my future. Though it was not expressed verbally, shortly after I began to work at their home, Jim became my mentor. He taught me a multitude of different things from how to do electrical work, to how to have better manners. I could not name all of the life lessons that I have learned, and am still learning, from this family. Presently I call him dad and we consider them as grandparents and their daughter as an aunt to our children. I never knew what the Lord would bring to me that day when I went to lunch, I thought I was just getting a free lunch, but I ended up forming priceless relationships. I challenge you to search for a mentor in your circle of influence, but always trusting God will bring to you who He wants as your mentor.

-Paul

CHALLENGE – Day 26

In being fatherless you will have both direct and indirect mentors. They can switch in and out at different points in your life. You may be closer to one more than the other. Direct mentors are those men that do things for you exactly at this moment. They know that they are trying to make a difference in your life as well. Indirect mentors are those men that you watch and begin to follow certain life patterns that they may possess in their lives. This could be a male employer, a pastor, a teacher, a coach, a relative, or someone else. The exciting thing about your situation is that you have the ability to pick up the best qualities of the mentors in your life. You have the chance to learn completely different things from each of them. Items such as: how to hunt, how to use money, how to treat girls, how to camp, how to work on cars, how to respect authority, and the list goes on. Some of the things you will learn will be a mixture of what a couple of your mentors will teach you. Having mentors can be fun if you make it that way. A key part in having mentors is accepting that you truly are fatherless and understanding that you cannot learn these things on your own. Do not fret, because there are men of God in your local community that will heed to the teaching of James 1:27 and similar passages, just continue to trust God until your mentor comes along.

 ACTION - In My Prayer Journal

Make a list of the men that you consider to be mentors or even potential mentors in your life. If you include a current mentor in your list write out the things that you think you could learn from that mentor. Make a list of things that this mentor has already taught you. If you include a possible mentor write out ways that you could try to become closer to them. An example of this would be to ask the potential mentor to teach you how to change oil in a car or if he wants to get together and talk. Don't be afraid to ask potential mentors questions about life. In doing so, it will bring you closer to them. Everything is worth a try. If you get turned down by a mentor, don't worry about it. Just pray and ask God that He will give you the mentor you are supposed to have. Sit back and watch how God works. He may give you a mentor, or He may even bring you closer to a family member or a current friend.

Suggested Prayer: Dear Lord, I pray trusting that You will work on a Christian man's heart to have the desire to teach me the things that I need to learn to become a man of You. Amen.

The Fatherless Journey

The Fatherless Journey

Day 27

Father's Day

"From the end of the earth will I cry unto thee, when my heart is overwhelmed: lead me to the rock that is higher than I." Psalm 61:2

One year, on Father's Day, at the end of the Church service, I ran out as quickly as possible. I thought that I was going to escape the misery that I was facing on yet another Father's Day. As I reached the exit door, my youth pastor called my name. He had seen my upset demeanor and wanted to make sure that I was okay. All I could do with the deep emotions that consumed me was begin to tear up. I told him in an angry manner how much I hated Father's Day. I explained to him that I did not think it was fair that I did not have a dad. My youth pastor calmed me down, as he did several times before. He explained to me that God was my Abba Father. I will not forget this day. I don't quite remember everything my youth pastor said to me, but I do remember the feeling of relief coming over me. I remember that day as a breaking point in my life. Finally someone besides my mom cared about me on Father's Day. Sure, I had mentors up to this point but no matter what, on Father's Day it would always pierce my heart that I had nothing to celebrate. I didn't have anyone to love. I did not have anyone to buy a gift or make things for. When the fathers stood up in church to be recognized, I would sit there sadly remembering that I didn't have a dad. When my Grandfather was alive I would honor him on Father's Day, but now he was gone and I felt all alone. I do not recommend this, but I remember times after my Grandfather died that we would skip church on Father's Day, because the pain was too great to bear. As I got older, God brought my current father figure into my life. It was so nice to have someone to honor, because before, Father's Day was just a reminder that I was fatherless. Now that I am a father myself and the lack of having a father has gotten much easier. I challenge you today to begin looking at fathers differently. The older you get the easier Father's Day will become. Remember that God is your Abba Father, and when all else fails, He is there for you to honor on Father's Day.

-Paul

CHALLENGE – Day 27

Everyone loves holidays! Most are filled with joy, happiness, and they sometimes even include a few days off of school or work. They are a time to share and reflect on the meaning of that special day. Christmas is a day to remember the Birth of Jesus Christ and Easter is when we remember His death, burial, and resurrection. Valentine's Day we take some extra time to express how we feel about the ones we like or love. On the Fourth of July we remember our independence in the United States of America and that we are free to live, and most importantly, that we have religious freedom. New Year's gives us a fresh slate to complete goals. There are many holidays throughout the year, but one that plagues the fatherless is Father's Day. For many fatherless individuals this day brings sadness and despair. For some it might be seen somewhat too overwhelming to bear. Whatever this day brings to you, you can get through it. In Psalm 61, David wrote, "From the end of the earth will I cry unto thee, when my heart is overwhelmed: lead me to the rock that is higher than I." Even David had days when he too was overwhelmed, but he trusted God to get him through those tough times. When you are feeling overwhelmed on Father's Day look to the Lord for strength and comfort.

 ## ACTION - In My Prayer Journal

Make a list of the reasons that Father's Day is hard for you. Pray daily that God will give you strength and comfort to get through the upcoming Father's Day and any other days that may overwhelm you.

Suggested Prayer: Dear Lord, I ask that You would please provide strength and comfort to me on Father's Day and other days that I feel overwhelmed. I realize that only through You can I get through these things, and I ask that You will lead me to the rock that is higher than I. Amen.

The Fatherless Journey

The Fatherless Journey

Day 28

Character

"A double minded man is unstable in all his ways." James 1:8
"There is therefore now no condemnation to them which are in Christ Jesus, who walk not after the flesh, but after the Spirit." Romans 8:1

When I was in junior high and high school, I had the opportunity to attend a good private Christian school. The principal of that school at the time was a nice guy and though I have not spoken to him personally in quite some time, I always considered him a friend. One thing that sticks out in my mind about him is that he constantly drilled into his students' minds the importance of having Christian character in our lives. I cannot tell you how many times he spoke on this subject, because it was quite often. One quote he would use when stressing the importance of character was: "There are two choices on the shelf, pleasing God and pleasing self." I do not think that he was the originator of this saying, but he quoted it often. Now that I am older I have grown to realize how important character is and how thankful I am that my principal was so repetitive in sharing this with us. Being fatherless we do not have as many boundaries as individuals usually do with fathers. It is important that we establish character in our personal lives so that we do not fall into serving the flesh or into one of Satan's traps. I challenge you today to be a man of character by living for the Lord and not for yourself!

–Paul

CHALLENGE – Day 28

What about you? Do you have character? If so, how much character do you have? Do you understand what character is? A simple definition would be: "character is what it takes to stop you." For example, what if you and a few friends were at the mall and one of your friends tempted you to steal a t-shirt from a store? You could do one of two things:

1. You could live for the flesh – and steal the shirt.
2. You could live for the Spirit – and tell your friends no, resist your flesh, and ultimately display your level of character.

Eventually as your character grew you would most likely not even be friends with individuals that tried to get you to do things like this. Our Savior, the Lord Jesus Christ was the epitome of character. He resisted the temptations of this world. He lived a consistent life of character until He was crucified on a cross for our sins. As Christians, we are to be striving to be "Little Christ's" in this world. Part of being "Little Christ's" contains striving to be a person of character. Strive today to be a young man of character by walking "not after the flesh, but after the Spirit."

 ACTION - In My Prayer Journal

Make a list of the things that you may struggle with in your life. The things that make you fall easily. Then write out the things that you have had recent success with. Begin trying to make the success list much larger than the struggles list by praying and striving to live for God.

Suggested Prayer: Dear Lord, please help me to be a man of character. Regardless of my situation I need to strive to live for You. Only though You will I be able to achieve true character. Amen.

The Fatherless Journey

82

The Fatherless Journey
Day 29

Work Ethic

"Servants, be obedient to them that are your masters according to the flesh, with fear and trembling, in singleness of your heart, as unto Christ; Not with eyeservice, as menpleasers; but as the servants of Christ, doing the will of God from the heart; With good will doing service, as to the Lord, and not to men: Knowing that whatsoever good thing any man doeth, the same shall he receive of the Lord, whether he be bond or free. And, ye masters, do the same things unto them, forbearing threatening: knowing that your Master also is in heaven; neither is there respect of persons with Him." Ephesians 6:5-9

As a teenager I had the opportunity to work a really cool job. I worked for my mentors two companies. The first company had four different carwashes and the second company had air machines and vacuums at gas stations and businesses all throughout Pennsylvania, Maryland, and West Virginia. After school on Tuesdays and Thursdays, it was my responsibility to drive to one of the carwashes that was located an hour and a half away. I was paid hourly for the drive and for the work I completed at the carwash. The work included spraying down the carwash floors, taking out the trash, collecting the money, etc. Included in this job was a lot of trust. I could have said I drove down there and never actually went. I could have driven down there, goofed off, and not completed all of the tasks. Now, do not get me wrong, I was not always perfect, but for the most part, I tried to have a good work ethic. One of the things that really kept me doing the work that I was supposed to do was that I imagined that there were hidden cameras and that I was being watched as I worked. During this entire time, even until this very moment, there was and is someone watching over me. God is Omnipresent, which means He is everywhere. I challenge you today to have a work ethic that is honoring and pleasing in the presence of God.

-Paul

CHALLENGE – Day 29

What type of responsibilities or "jobs" has God placed into your life at this very moment? Have you been doing your best or have you just been trying to get by? Remember that the chores currently in your life are God's current will for your life. Your job may be to complete chores around the house, or you may have a job with a business or with someone you know that pays a wage. Regardless, we are to strive for good work ethic. Being a Christian, you have a responsibility to have a good work ethic. It should be one of your top priorities to practice. Most likely people that you work with will know that you are a Christian. For many of your co-workers, you may be the only "Bible" that they will ever read. Pretend that there are cameras watching you as you work, because you are being watched. God is always watching you, as Paul said in Ephesians 6:5-9. He knows whether you are working or slacking. Some examples of good work ethic would be:

1. **Be at work on time.**
2. **Complete your tasks promptly and in order.**
3. **Give 100% to the job.**
4. **Submit and respect your authority.**
5. **Be cheerful.**
6. **Show a good testimony.**
7. **Have integrity and character.**
8. **Be a witness to others.**

I Corinthians 10:31 says "Whether therefore ye eat, or drink, or whatsoever ye do, do all to the glory of God." From this day forward begin to honor the Lord in everything that you do!

 ## ACTION - In My Prayer Journal

Write out the areas that you need to improve in your personal work ethic, whether it be getting to work on time, not complaining when asked to do something, working on your schoolwork as you should, helping your mother in whatever she needs, or whatever it may be. Then begin praying that God will help you improve and start today working on your list.

Suggested Prayer: Dear Lord, please help me to have good work ethic. Help me to serve You in whatever chore, task, project, or job I may be working on. Only through You will I be able to do this. Amen.

The Fatherless Journey

The Fatherless Journey

Day 30

Success

"I have fought a good fight, I have finished my course, I have kept the faith:
Henceforth there is laid up for me a crown of righteousness, which the Lord, the
Righteous Judge, shall give me at that day: and not to me only, but unto all them
also that love His appearing."
II Timothy 4:7-8

Congratulations! You made it! Today is the last day on the path to conquering your fatherless journey, and I want to be the first to congratulate you! You have done a great job, and I am very proud of you! You are on your way to having the ability to live a successful life! I am so excited that you made it over the fatherless mountain. I am sure you will agree that working through these issues was not the easiest thing that you have done, but they needed to be accomplished. I am proud of you for completing this devotional and sticking with it. When I was 23 years old I graduated from college with a Bachelor's Degree. This is a common life situation for many, but for me it was a huge success in my life. I had actually finished it. It was very hard with working 40+ hours a week and full time school, but I was able to complete it. All throughout college my theme verse was I Thessalonians 5:24 "Faithful is he that calleth you, who also will do it." Even to this day I remember a young man in high school saying the following to me: "You always say you are going to do stuff, but you never actually do." This was his response to me after I said that I was going to begin playing the guitar. Even though I had the intention to play the guitar, his statement for that situation was true, I never did learn how to play the guitar, but I have remembered his statement. Success is completing stuff you commit to, whether it is a job, relationship, chore, or whatever it may be. If you commit to something, strive to complete it. I challenge you today to continue on with success in your fatherless journey.

-Paul

CHALLENGE – Day 30

Noah's Ark and the story of the Flood have become known throughout the world. For many it is an intriguing story that people look at as fiction. Noah was a real man, and the flood that covered the earth actually did happen. Maybe they cannot comprehend giving of their lives to God to build an Ark that took several years. Maybe they cannot comprehend the fact that every man besides Noah's family was wiped off the face of the earth. It could be that they do not understand how one could save at least two of every kind of animal or that a boat could be built back then that would last through such a storm. There are many things concerning Noah's journey, the construction of the ark and the actual flood, that we may have a hard time understanding. Noah probably struggled with understanding it as well, but in the end, it was a success. Noah was not perfect, but he did what God had told him to do. He took the burden of a large problem upon his shoulders, and this is what Hebrews 11:7 says about him: "By faith Noah, being warned of God of things not seen as yet, moved with fear, prepared an ark to the saving of his house; by the which he condemned the world, and became heir of the righteousness which is by faith." What about you? Right now your flood is your fatherless situation, and you must not give up as you build the big boat to survive. You have to continue on with the project until it is complete. We pray at Life Factors Ministries that you will strive to grow strong in the Lord as you continue on in your fatherless journey.

 ACTION - In My Prayer Journal

Write out the things that you will need to continue to work through on your fatherless journey so that you will have true success. Pray, asking God to give you wisdom and guidance along your journey.

Suggested Prayer: Dear Lord, I thank You for giving me the ability to finish this devotional and life guide. I thank You for the lessons that You have taught me and I ask that You would please help me to live a successful life according to You. Amen.

The Fatherless Journey

MYFATHERLESSJOURNEY.ORG

Life Factors Ministries created myfatherlessjourney.org as a website specifically designed to meet the needs of all fatherless girls/guys, single moms/guardians, and mentors. We are here for you and want to help you along your fatherless journey! Check the site out today!

MY PRAYER JOURNAL

NAME

The Fatherless Journey

PRAYER JOURNAL INTRODUCTION

Every day of the fatherless journey you will be asked to take action and make an entry into this prayer journal. This journal will help you on your journey in many ways. After you have completed your 30 day fatherless journey you should refer back to your journal to watch the progress that you have been making in your life. As you will notice, as you go through this fatherless journey that prayer and trusting God are the most important tools that you will ever use.

The Fatherless Journey

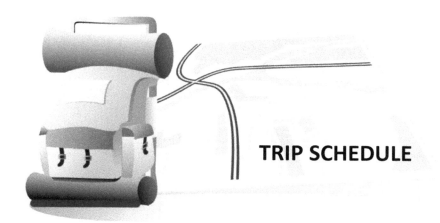

TRIP SCHEDULE

Preparation

Day 1 – Your Heavenly Father
Day 2 – So, You Are Fatherless
Day 3 – Facing the Facts
Day 4 – Talking to God
Day 5 – You Are Not Alone
Day 6 – You Are Loved
Day 7 – Consequences for Not Climbing
Day 8 – Overcoming Fear
Day 9 – Dealing with Discouragement

The Trip – Week 1 – The Incline (Internal Change)

Day 10 – Forgiveness
Day 11 – Inferiority
Day 12 – Trusting God
Day 13 – Uncontrolled Anger
Day 14 – Fearfully & Wonderfully Made
Day 15 – Self Esteem
Day 16 – Giving It All to God

The Trip – Week 2 – The Peak (External Change)

Day 17 – Submission to Authority
Day 18 – Man of God
Day 19 – Man of the House
Day 20 – A Lady's Man
Day 21 – Being the Leader
Day 22 – Learning From Example
Day 23 – Manhood without Guidance

The Trip – Week 3 – The Summit (Your Future)

Day 24 – Be Confident
Day 25 – Mentors Part 1
Day 26 – Mentors Part 2
Day 27 – Father's Day
Day 28 – Character
Day 29 – Work Ethic
Day 30 – Success

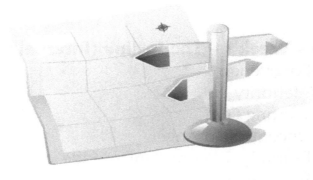

My Prayer Journal

Day 1 – Your Heavenly Father

Proverbs 3:5-6

 ACTION

In your first prayer journal entry write out a thank you letter to God for sending His Son to die for your sins.

My Prayer Journal

Day 2 – So, You Are Fatherless

Philippians 4:11

 ACTION

In the form below write out the things that you have in your life to be thankful for. Remember that your life can always be in a worse state than it currently is.

My Prayer Journal

Day 3 – Facing the Facts

Romans 8:17, 28

 ACTION

Write out a challenge for yourself of how you will not become one of the statistics. Challenge yourself with goals that can be easily accomplished. Continuously look back at your goals and confirm that you are still achieving them.

My Prayer Journal

Day 4 – Talking to God

James 5:16b

 ACTION

Write a note to God thanking Him for the things He has done and is doing in your life. Talk to Him about your burdens and problems. Look back at this note often and see what God has done in your life.

My Prayer Journal

Day 5 – You Are Not Alone

Hebrews 13:5

 ACTION

Make a list of the times you feel most alone. Begin to ask God to give you
strength and comfort in those times.

My Prayer Journal

Day 6 – You Are Loved

Galatians 2:20

 ACTION

Write a letter to Jesus thanking Him for what He has done for your life.

My Prayer Journal

Day 7 – Consequences for Not Climbing

Ephesians 5:14-17

 ACTION

Make a list of the top 5 things that you know God wants you to do with your life right now. Some examples would be: respecting your parents, climbing this mountain, living a pure life, giving 100% in school, witnessing to a friend, quitting a bad habit, etc.

My Prayer Journal

Day 8 – Overcoming Fear

II Timothy 1:7

 ACTION

Write out a list of all of your fears. Begin meditating on II Timothy 1:7 daily thinking of your fears, and ask God to help you conquer them.

My Prayer Journal

Day 9 – Dealing with Discouragement

Psalm 55:22

 ACTION

Make a list of the items you are currently discouraged about in your life. Pray over them and then begin praying for 30 days straight that God would deliver you from discouragement.

My Prayer Journal

Day 10 - Forgiveness

Ephesians 4:31-32

 ACTION

Make a list of the individuals in your life that you need to forgive. Begin to pray for them and ask God to forgive you for any bitterness, hatred, or anger that you may feel. Then daily seek his strength and guidance to love those that have hurt you.

My Prayer Journal

Day 11 - Inferiority

II Corinthians 3:5

 ACTION

Make a list of the items in your life that are lacking because of not having a dad. Then begin to pray daily that God will help you overcome your inferiority.

My Prayer Journal

Day 12 – Trusting God

Proverbs 3:5-6

 ACTION

Write out your victories and losses in life from the past few months. Then write out how you could better trust God through the losses and better praise Him in the victories.

My Prayer Journal

Day 13 - Uncontrolled Anger

Ephesians 4:26, 31

 ACTION

Write out the things or people in your life that make you angry. Also write out the things or people that you have bitterness towards. Begin praying about them and work on overcoming anger and bitterness.

My Prayer Journal

Day 14 – Fearfully & Wonderfully Made

Psalm 139:13-14

 ACTION

Write out the picture viewers would see if they watched your television show. Be honest. If there are items that you are not satisfied with, handle them as you can, and then give the rest to God. Try to daily improve your TV show as you continue on conquering the fatherless mountain!

My Prayer Journal

Day 15 – Self Esteem

I Timothy 4:12

 ACTION

Make a list of the positions you could be in: where you could be an example to your peers. Begin praying for these items, and ask God to help you be an example with high self-esteem.

My Prayer Journal

Day 16 – Give Your Life To God

Romans 14:7-9

 ACTION

Write out a letter to God telling Him the things in your life that you need and want to surrender to Him. Pray for those things that you have a hard time letting go of. Tell Him you give him your life and really mean it.

My Prayer Journal

Day 17 – Submission To Authority

Ephesians 6:1-3 & Romans 13:1-3

 ACTION

Write out the authority figures that are currently in your life. Then put an <u>R</u> beside the names that you feel you have respected or you do currently respect, and then put a <u>D</u> beside those names you have been disrespectful to. Work on trying to have all <u>R</u>'s within the next 30 days, despite how hard it may seem.

My Prayer Journal

Day 18 – Man of God

II Timothy 2:19

 ACTION

Write out anything that comes between you and God. Examples would be possessions, friends, sin, entertainment, or a variety of other things. Pray that God would help you to overcome these things and that He will help you to grow daily as a man of God.

My Prayer Journal

Day 19 – Man of the House

I Corinthians 7:24

 ACTION

Write out the responsibilities that you have been given due to being fatherless. Pray about them daily. If there are things you do not know how to do either research it on the internet or ask a male figure in your church, school, or family, to show you. You will never learn if you do not ask.

My Prayer Journal

Day 20 – A Lady's Man

I Corinthians 7:1 & Matthew 5:27-28

 ACTION

Write out a description of your ideal wife. Remember to include her desire to serve God, her appearance, her mindsets, her abilities, her strengths, her personality traits, and whatever else that may come to your mind that reflects a woman of God. Begin praying daily for this woman, asking God to prepare both you and her for your lives together.

My Prayer Journal

Day 21 – Being the Leader

Galatians 6:4

 ACTION

Make a list of the items in your life that you currently lead. Pray for the list and pray for the things that you will lead in the future.

My Prayer Journal

Day 22 – Learning By Example

I Corinthians 3:13-17

 ACTION

Write out certain bad and good characteristics about your father or other manly examples in your life. Begin praying that God will help you become the man that He wants you to be, excluding the bad things that your father or other examples may model.

My Prayer Journal

Day 23 – Manhood Without Guidance

Psalm 34:19

 ACTION

Make a list of 5 things that you wish you could have learned from your dad. Then begin to pray for them and that God would provide someone or some situation where you could learn them.

My Prayer Journal

Day 24 – Be Confident

II Corinthians 12:7-10

 ACTION

Make a list of the top 10 things in your life that seem to be impossible. Begin praying for these things daily until they are no longer impossible.

My Prayer Journal

Day 25 – Mentors Part I

Psalm 84:11

 ACTION

Make a list of the characteristics that you would look for in a mentor. For example you may want a man that will teach you how to hunt or how to fix a car. Begin praying that God will provide a Christian mentor that you can model your life after.

My Prayer Journal

Day 26 – Mentors Part II

James 1:27

 ACTION

Make a list of the men that you consider to be mentors or even potential mentors in your life. If you include a current mentor in your list write out the things that you think you could learn from that mentor. Make a list of things that this mentor has already taught you. If you include a possible mentor write out ways that you could try to become closer to them. An example of this would be to ask the potential mentor to teach you how to change oil in a car or if he wants to get together and talk. Don't be afraid to ask potential mentors questions about life. In doing so, it will bring you closer to them. Everything is worth a try. If you get turned down by a mentor, don't worry about it. Just pray and ask God that He will give you the mentor you are supposed to have. Sit back and watch how God works. He may give you a mentor, or He may even bring you closer to a family member or a current friend.

My Prayer Journal

Day 27 – Father's Day

Psalm 61:2

 ACTION

Make a list of the reasons that Father's Day is hard for you. Pray daily that God will give you strength and comfort to get through the upcoming Father's Day and any other days that may overwhelm you.

My Prayer Journal

Day 28 - Character

James 1:8 & Romans 8:1

 ACTION

Make a list of the things that you may struggle with in your life. The things that make you fall easily. Then write out the things that you have had recent success with. Begin trying to make the success list much larger than the struggles list by praying and striving to live for God.

My Prayer Journal

Day 29 – Work Ethic

Ephesians 6:5-9

 ACTION

Write out the areas that you need to improve on in your personal work ethic, whether it be getting to work on time, not complaining when asked to do something, working on your schoolwork as you should, helping your mother in whatever she needs, or whatever it may be. Then begin praying that God will help you improve and start today working on your list.

My Prayer Journal

Day 30 - Success

II Timothy 4:7-8

 ACTION

Write out the things that you will need to continue to work through on your fatherless journey so that you will have true success. Pray, asking God to give you wisdom and guidance along your journey.

MYFATHERLESSJOURNEY.ORG

Life Factors Ministries created myfatherlessjourney.org as a website specifically designed to meet the needs of all fatherless girls/guys, single moms/guardians, and mentors. We are here for you and want to help you along your fatherless journey! Check the site out today!

NOTES

1. Matthew Kinne in association with Snapdragon Group Editorial Services, *Fathers of Influence* (Colorado Springs: David C. Cook, 2006). 7.

2. U.S. Dept. of Justice, Special Report, Sept 1988.

3. US Dept. of Health & Human Services, Bureau of the Census.

4. National Principals Association Report on the State of High Schools.

5. Fulton Co. Georgia jail populations, Texas Dept. of Corrections, 1992.

6. Criminal Justice & Behavior, Vol 14, p. 403-26, 1978.

7. "Gilligans Island Theme Song," http://www.lyricsmode.com/lyrics/g/gilligans_island/gilligans_island_theme_song.html.

8. "Todd Beamer," http://en.wikipedia.org/wiki/Todd_Beamer.

9. "Vince Papale," http://en.wikipedia.org/wiki/Vince_Papale.

10. "Michael Jordan," http://en.wikipedia.org/wiki/Michael_Jordan.

11. "Abraham Lincoln," http://en.wikipedia.org/wiki/Abraham_Lincoln.

12. Joseph J. Ellis, *His Excellency: George Washington* (New York: Vintage Books, 2004). 7-10.

CPSIA information can be obtained
at www.ICGtesting.com
Printed in the USA
JSHW021153230120
3740JS00002B/4

9 780983 203957